About the Author

Birds have been an important part of Julie Rach Mancini's life ever since her father built a window shelf to feed pigeons as mealtime entertainment for her when she was a toddler. Her parents got her first bird, a parakeet named Charlie, when she was six, and she kept a special African grey parrot named Sindbad for more than ten years. Professionally, her interest in birds began to combine with her love of writing when the editors of *Pet Health News* asked her to write about bird health in 1988. She assisted in the preparation of the first issue of *Birds USA*, a successful annual publication aimed at the first-time pet bird owner, and became managing editor, then editor, of *Bird Talk* in 1992. Julie has been a freelance writer since 1997, with pets as her primary focus.

About Howell Book House

Since 1961, Howell Book House has been America's premier publisher of pet books. We're dedicated to companion animals and the people who love them, and our books reflect that commitment. Our stable of authors—training experts, veterinarians, breeders, and other authorities—is second to none. And we've won more Maxwell Awards from the Dog Writers Association of America than any other publisher.

As we head toward the half-century mark, we're more committed than ever to providing new and innovative books, along with the classics our readers have grown to love. This year, we're launching several exciting new initiatives, including redesigning the Howell Book House logo and revamping our biggest pet series, Your Happy Healthy Pet™, with bold new covers and updated content. From bringing home a new puppy to competing in advanced equestrian events, Howell has the titles that keep animal lovers coming back again and again.

Contents

Shopping List

You'll need to do a bit of stocking up before you bring your new bird home. Below is a basic list of some must-have supplies. For more detailed information on the selection of each item below, consult chapter 4. For specific guidance on what grooming tools you'll need, review chapter 7.

- ☐ Cage
- ☐ Open food and water bowls (at least two sets of each for easier dish changing and cage cleaning)
- ☐ Perches of various diameters and materials
- ☐ Sturdy scrub brush to clean the perches
- ☐ Food (a good quality fresh seed mixture or a formulated diet, such as pellets or crumbles)
- ☐ Millet spray (most cockatiels love this treat!)
- ☐ Powdered vitamin and mineral supplement to sprinkle on your pet's fresh foods
- ☐ A variety of safe, fun toys
- ☐ Cage cover (an old sheet or towel with no holes or ravels will serve this purpose nicely)
- ☐ Playgym (to give your cockatiel time out of his cage and a place to exercise)

There are likely to be a few other items that you're dying to pick up before bringing your bird home. Use the following blanks to note any additional items you'll be shopping for.

- ☐ ______________________________
- ☐ ______________________________
- ☐ ______________________________
- ☐ ______________________________
- ☐ ______________________________
- ☐ ______________________________
- ☐ ______________________________
- ☐ ______________________________
- ☐ ______________________________

Pet Sitter's Guide

We can be reached at (__)_____-________ Cellphone (__)_____-________

____

We will return on __________ (date) at __________ (approximate time)

Bird's Name ______________________________

Species, Age, and Sex ________________________

Important Names and Numbers

Vet's Name ____________________ Phone (__)_____-________

Address ______________________________

Emergency Vet's Name ________________ Phone (__)_____-________

Address ______________________________

Poison Control ________________________ (or call vet first)

Other individual to contact in case of emergency ________________

____

Care Instructions

In the first three blanks let the sitter know what to feed, how much, and when; when to give treats; and when and how to exercise the bird.

Morning ______________________________

____

Afternoon ______________________________

____

Evening ______________________________

____

Medications needed (dosage and schedule) ________________

____

Any special medical conditions ____________________

____

Grooming instructions ________________________

____

My bird's favorite playtime activities, quirks, and other tips __________

____

____

Your Happy Healthy Pet™

Cockatiel

2nd Edition

Julie Rach Mancini

Howell Book House™

This book is printed on acid-free paper. ♾

Howell Book House
Published by Wiley Publishing, Inc., Hoboken, New Jersey

For general information on our other products and services or to obtain technical support please contact our Customer Care Department within the U.S. at (800) 762-2974, outside the U.S. at (317) 572-3993 or fax (317) 572-4002.

Wiley also publishes its books in a variety of electronic formats. Some content that appears in print may not be available in electronic books. For more information about Wiley products, please visit our web site at www.wiley.com.

Library of Congress Cataloging-in-Publication Data:
Mancini, Julie R. (Julie Rach)
Cockatiel / Julie Rach Mancini. 2nd ed.
p. cm. -- (Your happy healthy pet)
ISBN-13: 978-0-471-74824-3 (cloth : alk. paper)
ISBN-10: 0-471-74824-2 (cloth : alk. paper)
1. Cockatiel. I. Title. II. Series.
SF473.C6R33 2006
636.6'8656 dc22 2005024167

Printed in the United States of America

10 9 8 7 6 5 4 3 2 1

2nd Edition

Book design by Melissa Auciello-Brogan
Cover design by Michael J. Freeland
Book production by Wiley Publishing, Inc. Composition Services

Part I

The World of the Cockatiel

The Cockatiel

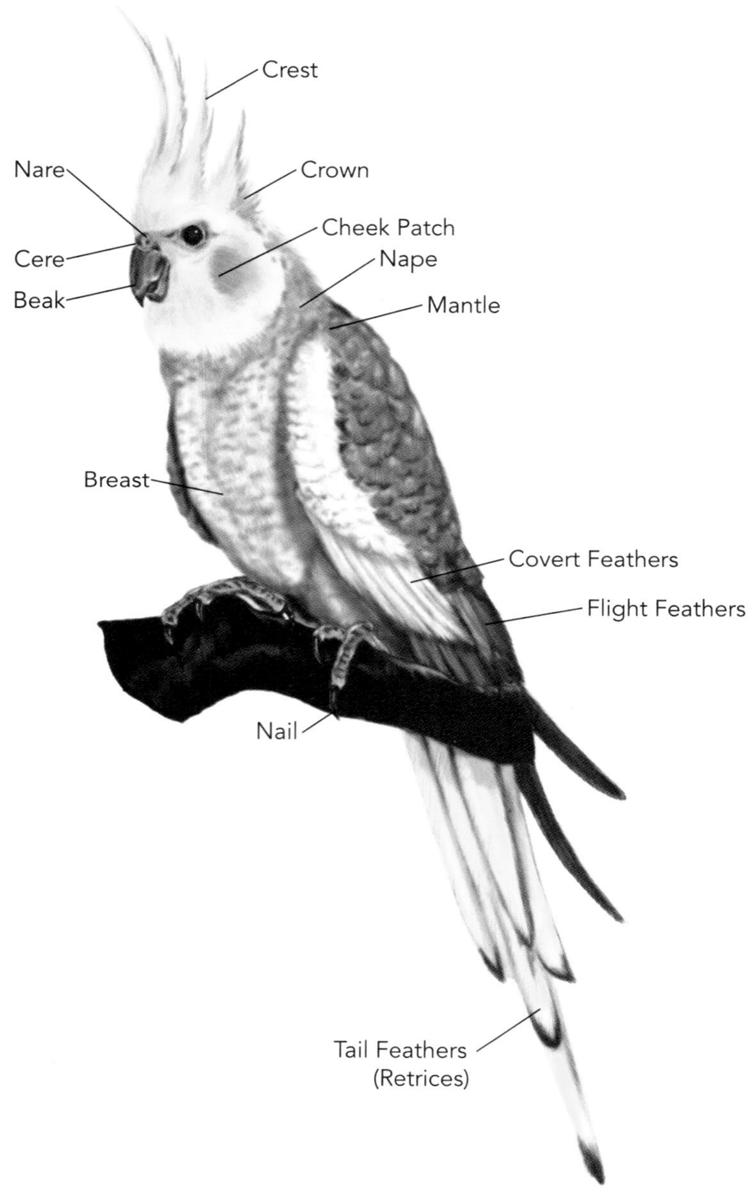

Chapter 1

What Is a Cockatiel?

Welcome to the wonderful world of cockatiels! For many people, cockatiels are their introduction to the fascinating hobby of birdkeeping. Some people move on to larger parrots after they become comfortable with caring for a cockatiel, while others specialize in raising cockatiels in pairs or small flocks. Still others show their cockatiels and achieve recognition for their birds' abilities to perform well in front of bird show judges.

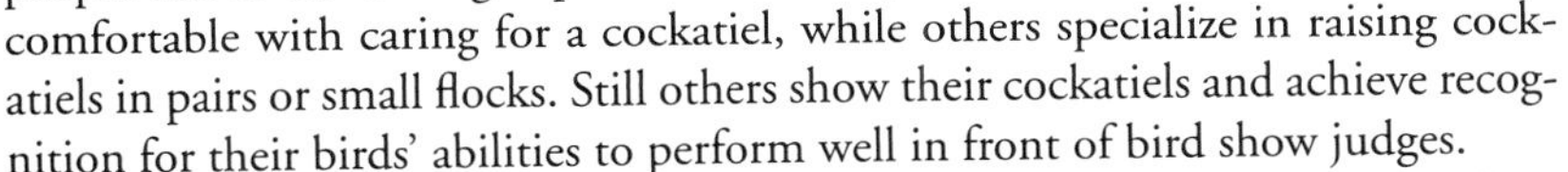

My first encounter with cockatiels was a bird named Stanley. Stanley eyed me curiously with one bright black eye from inside the small pet carrier. He was a young cockatiel on his way to Texas with a friend of mine. I had agreed to help socialize him to strangers before he made his big trip from the breeder's house to his new home.

I bent down by the carrier and talked to him softly, and he chirped a reply. My friend asked if I wanted to take him out of the carrier, which I did. I carefully opened the lid and Stanley hopped right out. I offered Stanley my hand as a perch. Again, he gave a careful look with one eye, then the other. After deciding it looked like a safe, sturdy place to sit, he climbed onto my finger. Stanley soon made his way up my arm and was nuzzling my neck. My appreciation for curious, affectionate cockatiels had begun.

Cockatiel Basics

Those of you who are new to pet birds are probably wondering just what a cockatiel is and what all the fuss is about. Let's meet one of the world's most popular pet birds, the cockatiel.

Parrot Traits

The cockatiel is a species of parrot, and all parrots have certain traits in common:

- Four toes on each foot—two pointing backward and two pointing forward
- The upper beak overhanging the lower beak
- Broad head and short neck

Cockatiels are long-tailed small parrots from Australia. They have been kept as pet birds for more than 160 years, since the first live birds were brought to Britain from Australia, and are second in popularity as pet parrots only to their Australian cousins, parakeets. The cockatiel is about twelve inches long, when you count those fabulous tail feathers, and comes in about a dozen colors and feather patterns.

Cockatiels make wonderful pets for individuals or families. Their size makes them appealing and approachable for children and adults.

Cockatiels offer their owners all the charm and personality of their larger cockatoo cousins without the inherent noise, biting, and other problems that come with the larger birds. Cockatiels are long lived (twenty years is not an uncommon life span), easy to maintain, and affordable to keep.

Although they are not particularly noted for their talking ability, most can learn to whistle simple tunes (the theme from *The Andy Griffith Show* seems to be a particular favorite for owners to teach their birds).

Thirty-four percent of bird-owning homes in America have a cockatiel, and these birds keep their owners entertained with their whistling ability and their comical antics. Through the years, cockatiels have helped educate schoolchildren about basic pet care in a classroom setting and brightened the lives of seniors and others in pet therapy programs.

In this book, I'll help you set up a healthy and interesting home for your cockatiel. You'll find out how to select a healthy bird, and I'll offer advice on feeding and grooming your pet. I will talk about the importance of regular veterinary care and look at some common cockatiel health problems. Finally, I'll look at normal cockatiel behaviors and offer some advice on how to teach your cockatiel to do tricks.

Why Choose a Bird?

Before you decide to bring a cockatiel into your life, you'll need to ask yourself a few questions. Do you like animals? Do you have time to care for one properly? Can you have pets where you live? Can you live with a little mess in your home (seed hulls, feathers, discarded food)?

If you answered yes to all these questions, you're a good candidate for bird ownership. Now think harder. Do you mind a little noise (cockatiels sometimes greet the dawn and bid adieu to the sunset with a song) as part of your daily routine? Are you allergic to dust and dander (some people find that cockatiels make them sneeze)? If the answer is no, a cockatiel may be just the bird for you!

Birds are extremely smart, and that means you will have to address your cockatiel's mental needs along with his physical needs.

Your next question might be, "Why do I want a bird?" Here are some of the answers.

Birds are relatively quiet pets. Unless you have a particularly vocal macaw or cockatoo, most birds aren't likely to annoy the neighbors the way a barking dog can. In the case of cockatiels, you'd need quite a large flock to disturb your neighbors because cockatiels have quiet, chirpy little voices. In many rental leases, birds may not even be considered pets because they are kept in a cage much of the time. This means you may be able to keep them without having to surrender a sizable security deposit to your landlord.

Birds interact well with their owners. Although a bird isn't as blindly loyal as the average dog, he is far more interactive than a fish, a hamster, or even a guinea pig. As an added bonus, many birds can learn to whistle or talk, which is unique among pets and which many bird owners find amusing and entertaining.

Birds are long-lived pets. A cockatoo named King Tut greeted visitors at the San Diego Zoo for seventy years, and *Bird Talk* magazine reported a 106-year-old Amazon parrot in Alaska. Many bird owners I know have made provisions for their larger parrots in their wills. Smaller birds can live long lives, too; the *Guinness Book of Records* lists an almost thirty-year-old parakeet in Great Britain.

TIP

If you're a bird owner who rents an apartment or house, you may be able to get your current landlord to write a letter of reference for your birds that you can use to show future landlords, explaining how responsible you are as a bird owner and how well behaved your bird has been.

The Right Reasons

Are you getting a cockatiel on a whim? Are you rescuing a bird from his aggressive cagemates? Are you buying a bird you feel sorry for? Noble though some of these reasons are, none of them is a good reason for getting a pet bird. Birds purchased for their pretty colors may soon be ignored or neglected by owners whose attention has been captured by another fancy. And small, timid birds may be hiding signs of illness that can be difficult and expensive to cure and that can cause you much heartache in the process.

Birds require consistent, but not constant, attention. This can be a plus for today's busy single people and families. While birds can't be ignored all day, they are content to entertain themselves for part of the day while their owners are busy elsewhere.

The needs and companionship of a bird provide a reason to get up in the morning. The value of this cannot be overestimated for older bird owners and single people who are on their own. Birds provide all the benefits of the human-animal bond, including lower blood pressure and reduced levels of stress.

Finally, birds are intelligent pets. Whoever coined the phrase "birdbrain" didn't appreciate how smart some birds are. On intelligence tests, some larger parrots have scored at levels comparable to chimpanzees, dolphins, and preschool-age children.

Cockatiels and Children

If you plan to get a cockatiel as a child's pet, please remember that children in the primary grades need some help from their parents or from older siblings to care for any pet. Children in the intermediate grades should be ready for the responsibility of bird ownership *with parental supervision*. Or the bird can just be a family pet, with each family member being responsible for some aspect of the bird's care. Even the youngest family members can help out by selecting healthy foods for the bird on a trip to the market or picking out a safe, colorful toy at the bird store.

Parents need to remind children of the following when they're around birds:

- Approach the cage quietly. Birds don't like to be surprised.
- Talk softly to the bird. Don't scream or yell at him.
- Don't shake or hit the cage.
- Don't poke at the bird or his cage with your fingers, sticks, pencils, or any other items.
- If you're allowed to take the bird out of his cage, handle him gently.
- Don't take the bird outside. In unfamiliar surroundings, birds can become confused and fly away from their owners. Most are never recovered.
- Respect the bird's need for quiet time.

I'd like to remind adults please not to give a live pet as a holiday present. Birthdays, Christmas, Hanukkah, Easter, and other holidays are exciting but stressful times for both people and animals. A pet coming into a new home is under enough stress just by joining his new family; don't add to his stress by bringing him home for a holiday. Instead, give your child pet-care accessories for the actual celebration and a gift certificate that will allow the child to select his or her pet (with parental supervision, of course) after the excitement of the special day has died down.

Cockatiel parents supervise their chicks, and you need to supervise your kids when they interact with a pet bird.

Chapter 2

The Cockatiel's History

Cockatiels have charmed many people. Some say it's their small size or affordable price that makes cockatiels so appealing, while others cite their appearance and personality. Some are captivated by the cockatiel's whistling abilities, cleanliness, and potentially long life span. And many bird owners are attracted to the cockatiel's curiosity and adaptability.

In any case, cockatiels can be wonderful pets who reward their owners with years of entertainment and companionship. In return for this love, a cockatiel requires care, attention, and understanding from you.

The Cockatiel's Background

The cockatiel originated in Australia, which is home to about fifty parrot species. In their homeland, cockatiels are sometimes called quarrion, weero, cockatoo parrot, or crested parrot. Small flocks of two to twelve birds gather together to live in Australia's interior, feeding on seedling grasses and other plants. Their habitats can range from open eucalyptus savannas to arid grasslands, and they are found across much of the Australian continent, except for coastal areas. (Only the parakeet and the rose-breasted cockatoo are found in as many parts of Australia as the cockatiel is.) Cockatiel flocks depend on rainfall for water. Once a steady supply of food and water are available, the breeding season begins.

The Cockatiel at a Glance

Native land: Australia

Also known as: quarrion, weero, cockatoo parrot, crested parrot

Length: about twelve inches from the top of the head to the end of the tail

Weight: 80 to 100 grams (2.8 to 3.5 ounces)

Life span: up to thirty-two years

Colors: Cockatiels come in a wide variety of colors. Their native or "wild" color is gray. From that, breeders have developed several mutations, including cinnamon (cinnamon-colored body feathers instead of the normal gray), albino (completely white body feathers with pink feet and red eyes), silver (silver to whitish body feathers), fallow (grayish-yellow body feathers and red eyes), lutino (light-yellow body feathers), pearl (scalloped wing feathers instead of solid-colored ones), pied (a mix of yellow, white, and gray body feathers), whiteface (a white face instead of the normal yellow with orange cheek patches), and yellowface (a very faint yellow cheek patch).

In the wild, cockatiels are active in the early morning and late afternoon. These are the times they usually head toward a water source to drink, being sure to leave quickly rather than become a meal for a passing bird of prey. They spend a good bit of their day on the ground searching for food, but they are likely to spend midday blending into their surroundings by sitting lengthwise along dead tree branches that are free of foliage. That's when their natural gray coloration comes in handy, because they blend in better with the surroundings than other, more brightly colored birds do.

No Imported Cockatiels

Although many parrot species were imported into North America from their native lands until the late 1980s, cockatiels have not been exported from Australia since 1894. All cockatiels sold as pets in the United States and Canada are domestically bred and raised, which makes them better pets than wild-caught animals.

A Link to Dinosaurs?

In 2001, scientists announced that a 130-million-year-old feathered dinosaur fossil had been discovered in China. It was the first dinosaur found with its body covering intact, and it was identified as a Dromaeosaur, a small, fast-running dinosaur closely related to Velociraptor, with a sickle claw on the middle toe and stiffening rods in the tail. According to the American Museum of Natural History, Dromaeosaurs are advanced theropods, which is a group of two-legged predators that includes Tyrannosaurus rex. Dromoaesaurs had sharp teeth and bones that are very similar to those of modern-day birds.

The fossil was found in Liaoning Province in northeastern China. It was described as looking like a large duck with a long tail. The animal's head and tail were covered with downy fibers, and it had other featherlike structures on the back of its arms and on other parts of its body.

The first feathered dinosaur was found in China in 1995. This discovery, Sinosauropteryx, was also a theropod dinosaur, and it was also found in Liaoning Province. Sinosauropteryx dates from between 121 and 135 million years ago, and it falls in between Archaeopteryx, the earliest known bird, which lived about 150 million years ago, and Protarchaeopteryx robusta, which lived at about the same time as Sinosauropteryx but probably could not fly, despite the presence of feathers on its body.

The cockatiel was first described by naturalists who visited Australia with Captain James Cook in 1770, and the first specimen may have come to the Royal College of Surgeons Museum in London as a result of this trip. Cockatiels were recorded as being kept in captivity in Europe by the 1840s, and their popularity as pets began to rise about forty years later. By the 1940s, they had

Several other species of feathered dinosaurs have been found in the same region, and scientists believe that some species of dinosaurs developed feathers to help them keep warm.

Fossils of birdlike dinosaurs and dinosaur-like birds have been found in Madagascar, Mongolia, and Patagonia, as well as in China. The *Eoalulavis*, found in Spain, was one of the earliest birds that could maneuver well during flight, thanks to a feather tuft on its thumb called an alula. This feature is found on birds today, and it helps them with takeoffs and landings. Some scientists theorize that birds evolved from dinosaurs, while others are still seeking an earlier reptile ancestor for birds.

Can't see this bird's resemblance to a dinosaur? Just look at her feet!

overtaken parakeets in popularity worldwide, but cockatiels dropped back to second place in the 1950s, where they have remained ever since.

The Australian government imposed a ban on exporting all native birds in 1894, so the cockatiels kept in North America and Europe have resulted from domestic breeding efforts in those countries for more than 100 years.

Wild cockatiels are gray. All the other colors are called mutations, and came as the result of controlled breeding.

Cockatiels have been kept in captivity about as long as parakeets have (since the 1830s). For the first 100 years or so, cockatiels were available in one color—gray—while parakeets began to be available in a variety of colors. Cockatiel breeders only began developing color mutations in their birds in the late 1940s, and now nine mutations are available: lutino, cinnamon, albino, silver, pied, fallow, pearl, whiteface, and yellowface. Breeders have also combined these mutations into almost infinite varieties and are developing new ones all the time.

How the Cockatiel Got Her Name

The cockatiel has been classified into her own genus, *Nymphicus,* and has her own species name, *hollandicus.* The scientific name, which went through several variations before a naturalist named Wagler settled on the present form in 1832, translates literally to "goddess of New Holland," which is the name Australia was known by in the 1700s and 1800s.

The first cockatiel color mutation (a color other than one that exists in wild birds) was the pied, which was first seen in California in 1949. The pied mutation results in blotches of color on a mostly white or mostly light-colored bird.

The cockatiel's name in English comes from either the Dutch *kakatielje,* which means "little cockatoo," or the Portuguese *cocatilho,* which means "small parrot."

Chapter 3

Choosing Your Cockatiel

Now that you know a little more about the history of the cockatiel, you'll need to know how to select the healthy, happy cockatiel who is the right pet for you. You'll need to think about whether you want a single bird or a pair, and whether a male or a female is right for you.

You'll also need to think about the cost of owning a cockatiel—in both time and money. To maintain his lovable personality, a cockatiel needs companionship. If you can't devote about a half hour every day to paying attention to your bird, either don't adopt him or make sure he has a cockatiel companion. That half hour could be spent cuddling on the couch while you watch TV, eating breakfast or dinner together, or having your bird on a playgym in your bedroom while you get ready in the morning. You can also spend time with your bird while making safe toys for him (such as stringing Cheerios or raw pasta on some bird-safe, vegetable-tanned leather), teaching him tricks, or building him a playgym.

The box on page 22 explains more about the commitment you'll need to make. If, after considering all these factors, you still want to add a cockatiel to your family because you want a cheerful companion, please read on to learn more about bringing a cockatiel into your life.

Where to Get Your Cockatiel

There are several ways you can get a cockatiel, including classified newspaper ads, bird shows, and pet stores. Let's look at the pros and cons of each in detail.

Classified Ads

Private parties who want to sell pet birds usually place classified ads. If the advertiser offers young birds, it is likely to be a private breeder who wants to place a few birds in good homes. Some breeders may also offer older birds for sale from time to time. These are most likely breeder birds who are too old to produce chicks but who are still good candidates for pet homes.

If you buy your bird from a private breeder, you will probably be shown only the birds the breeder has for sale. Do not be offended if you can't see all the birds; some are more sensitive than others about the presence of strangers during breeding season, and the sensitive ones may destroy eggs or kill chicks when they're upset. Cockatiels are less prone to this sensitivity than larger parrots, but a breeder may keep all of their nesting pairs in the same area. If, however, a breeder is willing to show you around their facility, consider it a special treat.

Bird Shows

Shows offer bird breeders and buyers an opportunity to get together to share a love for birds. Bird shows can give you the chance to see many different types of birds (usually far more than many pet shops keep at a time) all in one place, which can help you narrow your choices if you're undecided about which species to keep. At a bird show, you can see which birds win consistently, then talk to the breeder of these birds after the show to see if they are expecting any chicks.

At bird shows, you can see which birds win the ribbons and then talk to their breeders about getting a chick.

Pet Stores

Pet stores can be a good place to buy a cockatiel, but you must you do some checking first. You'll need to start by visiting the store to make sure it's clean and well kept. Walk around a bit. Are the floors clean? Do the cages look and smell as if they're cleaned regularly? Do the animals in the cages appear alert, well fed, and healthy? Do the cages appear crowded or do the animals inside have some room to move around?

The Bottom Line

Keeping a companion bird is a big responsibility. Here are some things you need to think about as you become a cockatiel owner.

- The cost of the bird
- The cost of his cage and accessories
- The cost of bird food (seeds, formulated diet, and fresh foods)
- The cost of toys
- The cost of veterinary care
- The amount of time you can devote to your bird each day
- How busy your life is already
- Who will care for the bird when you go on vacation or are away on business
- How many other pets you already own
- The size of your home

After you've determined that the store is clean and the employees are pleasant, find out what the staff does to keep their birds healthy. Do they ask you to wash your hands with a mild disinfectant before or between handling their birds? If they do, don't balk at the request. This is for the health of the birds and it indicates that the store is concerned about keeping its livestock healthy. Buying a healthy bird is much easier and more enjoyable than purchasing a pet with health problems, so look for a caring store and follow the rules.

If something about the store, staff, or birds doesn't feel quite right, take your business elsewhere. If the store and its birds meet with your approval, then it's time to get down to the all-important task of selecting your cockatiel.

Selecting Your Cockatiel

Once you've located a source for hand-fed cockatiels, it's time to get down to selecting your pet. First, observe the birds available for sale. If possible, sit down and watch them for a while. Take note of which birds seem bolder than the others. Consider those first, because you want a curious, active, robust pet, rather than a shy animal who hides in a corner.

TIP

You should try to acquire a young hand-fed cockatiel, if possible. A young cockatiel is weaned and eating on his own when he is about eight weeks old. Most breeders and pet stores have quite a few young birds available from April to September.

If possible, let your cockatiel choose you. Many pet stores display their cockatiels in colony situations on playgyms, or a breeder may bring out a clutch of babies for you to look at. If one bird waddles right up to you and wants to play, or if one comes over to check you out and just seems to want to come home with you, he's the bird for you!

Hand-Fed or Parent-Raised?

Regardless of where you buy your cockatiel, try to find a hand-fed bird. Although they cost a bit more than parent-raised ones, hand-fed cockatiels have been raised by people. This process emphasizes the bird's pet qualities and ensures that he will bond with people. You must be willing to spend time playing with and handling your hand-fed cockatiel every day to keep him tame.

Parent-raised chicks may require extra handling and care to become cuddly, easy-to-handle pets so they are better candidates for breeding programs. As their name suggests, parent-raised birds have imprinted on their parents as primary

Birds who were hand fed as chicks pay more attention to their human companions. (And the appearance of cockatiel chicks offers more evidence of birds' links with dinosaurs!)

Signs of Good Health

Here are some of the signs that a cockatiel is healthy. Keep them in mind when you are selecting your pet.

- Bright eyes
- A clean cere (the area above the bird's beak that covers his nares, or nostrils)
- Clean legs and vent
- Smooth feathers
- Upright posture
- A full-chested appearance
- Bird is actively moving around the cage
- Good appetite

caregivers and will act like birds when it comes time to raise chicks. Hand-fed pets, however, may pay more attention to their human companions than to other birds, so they may not make ideal candidates for breeding situations.

Male or Female?

You may be asking, "Should I get a male or a female cockatiel?" Generally speaking, male birds are more vocal and outgoing, while females have gentler natures. Although males may be slightly better talkers, I'd encourage you to get a young, healthy bird of either sex and enjoy your companion for his full pet potential.

If you are getting an adult bird, you can tell them apart by the brighter orange cheek patches in males. This won't work, of course, on color mutations that lack orange cheek patches.

One or Two?

Another question you may have (especially if you have a busy schedule) is, "Should I get one bird or two?" Single cockatiels generally make more affectionate pets, because you and your family become the bird's substitute flock. But a pair of cockatiels can be pretty entertaining as they encourage each other into all sorts of avian mischief. And if you are away from home all day every day, your two birds will keep each other company.

One small drawback of owning two pet cockatiels, especially young ones, is that they may have a tendency to chase each other around the cage, playfully

Some cockatiels enjoy the company of other birds, but some do not. If you really want more than one bird, it's best to bring them both home at the same time.

tugging on one another's tail feathers. Sometimes these feathers come out, leaving you with two considerably shorter cockatiels until the next set of tail feathers grows in. If you have a pair of birds who suddenly become tailless, check the cage bottom for the feathers and watch your birds to see if they do, indeed, chase and pester each other. If so, you have nothing to worry about. If not, please alert your avian veterinarian to the problem and ask for further guidance.

Two birds are also less likely to learn to talk to you, because they can chatter to each other in cockatiel rather than learning the language of their substitute human "flock."

If you do not bring both birds home at the same time, there is a possibility of territorial behavior on the part of the original bird. This territorial behavior can include bullying the newcomer and keeping him away from food and water dishes to the point where the new bird cannot eat or drink.

To avoid this problem, house the birds in separate cages and supervise all their interactions. Let the birds out together on a neutral playgym and watch how they act with each another. If they seem to get along, you can move their cages closer together so they can become accustomed to being close. Some birds will adjust to having other birds share their cages, while others prefer to remain alone in their cages with other birds nearby.

By the same token, don't try to put a new cockatiel into the cage of a bird you already own and don't house cockatiels with other small birds, such as finches, canaries, or lovebirds. Cockatiels may bully other small birds and keep them away from food and water bowls.

To keep peace in your avian family, make sure every bird has his own cage, food, and water bowls. Some cockatiels will get along with other birds during supervised time on a playgym, while others do not work and play well with others and enjoy being the only pets out on the gym.

Bringing Your Cockatiel Home

Although you will probably want to start playing with your new cockatiel the minute you bring him home, please resist this temptation. Your pet will need some time to adjust to his new environment, so be patient. Give your cockatiel a chance to gradually get used to your family. After you set your cockatiel up in his cage for the first time, spend a few minutes talking quietly to your new pet, and use his name frequently while you're talking. Describe the room he's living in, or tell him about your family. Move slowly around your cockatiel for the first few days to avoid startling him.

You will be able to tell when your new pet has settled into his routine. By observation, you will soon recognize your cockatiel's routine and know what is normal. You may also notice that your bird fluffs or shakes his feathers to greet you, or that he chirps a greeting when you uncover his cage in the morning. If your cockatiel learns to talk, he may eventually greet you with a cheery "hello" or "good morning" as you uncover his cage.

Don't become alarmed the first time you see your cockatiel asleep. Although it seems that your bird has lost his head or a leg, he's fine. Sleeping on one foot with his head tucked under his wing (actually, with his head turned about 180 degrees and his beak tucked into the feathers on the back of his neck) is normal for many parrots, although it looks a bit unusual or uncomfortable to bird owners. Be aware, too, that your bird will occasionally perch on one leg while resting the other.

It is very important to have a radio or television on for your cockatiel if you leave him home alone for long periods of time. Although cockatiels have been kept as pets for many years, they still retain many of their wild instincts. In the grasslands of Australia, silence usually indicates a predator is in the area, which can raise a bird's stress level and may make him more susceptible to illness.

Quarantine

If you have other birds in your home, you will want to quarantine your cockatiel for at least thirty days to ensure he doesn't have any diseases that your other birds could catch. To do this, you will need to keep your cockatiel as far away from your other birds as possible, preferably in a separate room. Feed your newly arrived cockatiel after you feed your other birds, and be sure to wash your hands thoroughly before and after handling or playing with your new pet.

Part II

Caring for Your Cockatiel

Chapter 4

Home Sweet Home

Before you bring your feathered friend home, you have a lot of shopping to do. Selecting your cockatiel's cage will be one of the most important decisions you make for her. You must also decide where she will live in your house or apartment. Don't wait until you bring your bird home to think this through. You'll want your new pet to settle in comfortably right away, rather than adding to her stress by relocating her several times before you decide on the right spot for the cage.

Choosing a Cage

When selecting a cage for your cockatiel, make sure the bird has room to spread her wings without touching the cage sides. Her tail should not touch the cage bottom, nor should her crest brush the top. A cage that measures eighteen-by-eighteen-by-twenty-four inches is the minimum size for a single cockatiel, and bigger is always better. If you are planning to keep a pair of birds, the cage should be at least twenty-four-by-twenty-four-by-forty inches.

Simply put, buy the largest cage you can afford because you don't want your cockatiel to feel cramped. Remember, too, that any parrot is like a little airplane, which means she flies *across* an area, rather than a little helicopter hovering up and down. For this reason, long, rectangular cages that offer horizontal space for short flights are better than high, tall cages that don't provide much flying room.

Wire Cages

Chances are you'll select a wire cage for your cockatiel. Some cages are sold as part of a cockatiel start-up kit, while others are sold separately. Discuss your options with the salesperson at your local pet supply store. Find out what advantages there are to purchasing a complete kit.

Regardless of whether it's part of a kit, carefully examine any cage you choose before making your final selection. Make sure the finish is not chipped, bubbled, or peeling, because your pet may find the spot and continue removing the finish, which can cause a cage to look old and worn before its time. Also, your bird could become ill if she ingests any of the finish.

Make sure the bar spacing on your cockatiel's cage is appropriate. The bars on this cage may be spaced too wide to keep this bird safely inside.

Reject any cages that have sharp interior wires or wide spaces between the bars. (Recommended bar spacing for cockatiels is about half an inch.) Sharp wires could poke your bird, she could become caught between bars that are slightly wider than recommended, or she could escape through widely spaced bars. Finally, make sure the cage you choose has some horizontal bars in it so your cockatiel can climb the cage walls easily for exercise.

Cage Door Options

Once you've checked the bar spacing and the overall cage quality, your next concern should be the cage door. Does it open easily for you, yet remain secure enough to keep your bird in her cage when you close the door? Will your bird's food bowl or a bowl of bath water fit through it easily? Is it long and wide enough for you to get your hand in and out of the cage comfortably—with the bird perched on your finger? (Remember, cockatiels have high crests and long tails!)

Does the door open up, down, or to the side? Some bird owners like their pets to have a play porch on a door that opens out and down, drawbridge style, while others are happy with doors that open to the side. Watch out for guillotine-style doors that slide up and over the cage entrance, because some cockatiels have suffered a broken leg when the door dropped on them unexpectedly.

Cage Considerations

Your cockatiel will spend much of her time in her cage, so make this environment as stimulating, safe, and comfortable as possible. Keep the following things in mind when choosing a cage for your cockatiel.

- Make sure the cage is big enough. The dimensions of the cage (height, width, and depth) should add up to at least sixty inches for a single bird.
- An acrylic cage may be easier to clean up. Wood or bamboo cages will be quickly destroyed by an eager cockatiel's beak.
- Make sure the cage door opens easily and stays securely open and closed. Avoid guillotine-style doors.
- The cage tray should be a regular shape and easy to slide in and out. There should be a grille below the cage floor so you can change the substrate without worrying about the bird escaping.

A door that opens to the side can make a nice perch for your bird.

Finally, check the floor of the cage you've chosen. Does it have a grille that will keep your bird out of the debris that falls to the bottom of the cage, such as feces, seed hulls, molted feathers, and discarded food? To ensure your cockatiel's long-term health, it's best to have a grille between your curious pet and the remains in the cage tray. It's also easier to keep your cockatiel in her cage while you're cleaning the cage tray if there's a grille between the cage and the tray.

What About Acrylic Cages?

Birdcages are traditionally made of metal wire, but you may see acrylic cages in magazine advertisements or at your local pet store. These cages are better at containing seed hulls, loose feathers, and other debris your bird creates, which may make birdkeeping easier and more enjoyable for you. Although it sounds like a sales pitch, I can attest to the fact that acrylic cages clean up easily by wiping inside and out with a damp towel and regularly changing the paper in the tray that slides under the cage itself.

If you choose an acrylic cage for your pet, make sure it has numerous ventilation holes drilled in its walls to allow for adequate air circulation. Be particularly careful about not leaving your cockatiel in direct sunlight if you house her in an acrylic cage, because these cages can get warm rather quickly and your bird could become overheated. (Cockatiels in wire cages shouldn't be left in direct sunlight either, as they can also overheat.) If you select an acrylic cage for your cockatiel, make sure to include a couple of ladders between the perches to give your pet climbing opportunities she won't be able to take advantage of on the smooth sides of an acrylic cage.

CAUTION

No Bamboo

If you find wooden or bamboo cages during your shopping excursions, reject them immediately. A busy cockatiel beak will make short work of a wooden or bamboo cage, and you'll be left with the problem of finding a new home for your pet! These cages are designed for finches and other songbirds, who are less likely than a cockatiel to chew on their homes.

The Cage Cover

One important, but sometimes overlooked, accessory is the cage cover. Be sure you have something to cover your cockatiel's cage with when it's time to put your bird to sleep each night. The act of covering the cage seems to calm many pet birds and convince them that it's really time to go to bed, despite the sounds of an active family evening in the background.

Consider getting a travel crate for your bird, for her annual checkup trips to the avian veterinarian.

You can purchase a cage cover or you can use an old sheet, blanket, or towel that is clean and free of holes. Be aware that some birds like to chew on their cage covers through the cage bars. If your bird does this, replace the cover when it becomes too tattered to do its job effectively. Replacing a well-chewed cover will also help keep your bird from becoming entangled in the cover or caught in a ragged clump of threads. Some birds have injured themselves quite severely by being caught in a chewed cage cover, so help keep your pet safe from this hazard.

Cockatiels may also benefit from a night-light left on for them at bedtime. Some cockatiels are prone to night frights, in which they thrash around the cage and can injure themselves quite seriously. Having a low-wattage light on helps these birds find their way around the cage at night, which may make them less prone to being startled.

What to Put in the Cage Tray

It is recommended that you use clean black-and-white newsprint, paper towels, or clean sheets of used computer printer paper. Sand, ground corncobs, or walnut shells may be sold by your pet supply store, but are not recommended as cage flooring materials because they tend to hide feces and discarded food quite well. This can cause a bird owner to forget to change the cage tray on the principle that if it doesn't look dirty, it must not be dirty. This line of thinking can set up a thriving, robust colony of bacteria in the bottom of your bird's cage, which can lead to a sick bird if you're not careful. Newsprint and other paper products don't hide the dirt; in fact, they seem to draw attention to it, which leads conscientious bird owners to keep their pets' homes scrupulously clean.

You may see sandpaper or "gravel paper" sold in some pet stores as a cage tray liner. This product is supposed to provide a bird with an opportunity to ingest grit, which is purported to aid indigestion by providing coarse grinding material that helps break up food in the bird's gizzard. However, many avian experts do not believe that a pet bird needs grit, and if a bird stands on rough sandpaper, it could cause foot problems. For your pet's health, please don't use these gravel-coated papers.

Location, Location

Now that you've picked the perfect cage for your pet, where will you put it in your home? Your cockatiel will be happiest when she's part of the family, so the living room, family room, or dining room may be among the best places for your bird. If your cockatiel is a child's pet, she may do well living in her young owner's room. (Parents should check on the bird regularly, though, to make sure she's being fed and watered and that her cage is clean.)

Avoid keeping your bird in the bathroom or kitchen, though, because sudden temperature fluctuations or fumes from cleaning products used in those rooms could harm your pet. Another spot to avoid is a busy hall or entryway, because the activity level in these spots may be too much for your pet. Set up the cage so that it's at your eye level if possible, because it will make taking care of the cage and visiting with your pet easier for you. It will also reduce the stress on your cockatiel, because birds like to be up high for security.

Every creature likes to feel secure when she's at home.

Setting up the Cage

Make sure you have the cage all set up and ready before you bring your bird home, to help ease the transition for your pet. Here's how to set up your cockatiel's cage.

- **Select the right location.** Your cockatiel will be more comfortable if her cage is set up in a part of the house that you and your family use regularly, such as a family room. Your cockatiel's cage should be out of the main traffic flow of the room, but still part of the room so you can include your bird in normal activities, such as watching TV. (Don't put your bird's cage near the kitchen or bathroom, because cooking and chemical fumes from these rooms can harm your cockatiel.)
- **Set the cage up with a solid wall behind it.** Your cockatiel will feel more secure if she has a solid wall behind her cage because nothing can sneak up on her from behind.
- **Stagger the perches within the cage.** Don't place the perches at all the same height in the cage because your cockatiel will be

They also do not like to have people or things looming over them, so please don't place your bird near items such as ceiling fans, chandeliers, or swag lamps. If members of your family are particularly tall, they may want to sit next to the cage or crouch down slightly to talk to the cockatiel.

Regardless of the room you select for your cockatiel, be sure to put the cage in a secure corner (with one solid wall behind the cage to give your cockatiel a sense of security); near a window is recommended. Please don't put the cage in direct sun, though, because cockatiels can quickly overheat.

More to Buy

Along with the perfect size cage in the ideal location in your home, your cockatiel will need a few cage accessories. These include food and water dishes, perches, and toys.

Food and Water Dishes

You want the dishes to be easy to clean and heavy enough so that when your bird perches on the edge, they will not tip. Cockatiels seem to enjoy food crocks, which happier if she can perch at different heights at different times of the day.

- **Arrange the perches correctly.** Don't place perches directly over food or water bowls because pet birds eliminate regularly during the day, and you don't want your pet's food or water contaminated by her droppings.
- **Add some toys.** Your cockatiel will need toys in her cage to help entertain her during the day. You should rotate the toys regularly to ensure your bird doesn't become bored with the same toys. You'll also have to replace those that your pet destroys during playtime. Don't overfill the cage with toys because your bird still needs room to move around. She needs to climb around in the cage and maybe even take short flights from end to end for exercise. She also needs to be able to get to the food and water bowls without interference from her toys.
- **Provide a cage cover.** Your cockatiel will benefit from having her cage covered when she goes to sleep at night. Covering the cage will help your bird settle down at bedtime, which helps her establish a good daily routine.

are open ceramic bowls that they can hop up on the edge of and pick and choose what they will eat during the day. Be sure to buy shallow dishes that are less than one inch deep to ensure that your bird has easy access to her food at all times.

When buying dishes for your cockatiel, be sure to pick up several sets so that mealtime cleanups are quick and easy. Never buy plastic dishes, because the pores in plastic can harbor bacteria even when the dishes are washed daily.

Perches

When choosing perches for your pet's cage, try to buy at least two different diameters of materials so your bird's feet won't get tired of standing on the same-size perch made of the same material day after day. Think of how tired your feet would feel if you stood on a piece of wood in your bare feet all day, then imagine how it would feel to stand on that piece of wood barefoot every day for ten or fifteen years. Sounds pretty uncomfortable, doesn't it? That's basically what your bird has to look forward to if you don't vary her perching choices.

The recommended diameter for cockatiel perches is five-eighths of an inch, so try to buy one perch that size and one slightly larger (three-quarters of an inch, for example) to give your pet a chance to stretch her foot muscles. Birds spend almost all of their lives standing, so keeping their feet healthy is important. Also,

Perches of different sizes and uneven ones made of natural wood will help keep your bird's feet healthy.

avian foot problems are much easier to prevent than they are to treat.

You'll probably notice a lot of different kinds of perches when you visit your pet supply store. Along with the traditional wooden dowels, bird owners can now buy perches made from manzanita branches, and PVC tubes, rope perches, and terra-cotta or concrete grooming perches.

Manzanita offers birds varied diameters on the same perch, along with chewing possibilities, while PVC is almost indestructible. (Make sure any PVC perches you offer your bird have been scuffed slightly with sandpaper to improve traction.) Rope perches also offer varied diameter and a softer perching surface than wood or plastic, and terra-cotta and concrete provide slightly abrasive surfaces that birds can use to groom their beaks without severely damaging the skin on their feet in the process. However, some bird owners have reported that their pets have suffered foot abrasions with these perches, so if you choose to use them, watch your pet carefully for signs of sore feet (an inability to perch or climb; favoring a foot; or raw, sore skin on the feet). If your bird shows signs of lameness, remove the abrasive perches immediately and arrange for your avian veterinarian to examine her.

No Sandpaper, Please

To help your bird avoid foot problems, do not use sandpaper covers on her perches. These abrasive sleeves, touted as nail trimming devices, really do little to trim a parrot's nails because birds don't usually drag their nails along their perches. What the sandpaper perch covers are good at doing, though, is abrading the surface of your cockatiel's feet, which can leave her vulnerable to infections and can make movement painful.

When placing perches in your bird's cage, try to vary the heights slightly so your bird has different levels in her cage. Don't place any perches over food or water dishes, because birds will contaminate food or water by eliminating in it. Finally, place one perch higher than the rest for a nighttime sleeping roost. Cockatiels and other parrots like to sleep on the highest point they can find to perch, so please provide this security for your pet.

Choosing the Right Toys

Cockatiels need toys to occupy their minds, bodies, and beaks. Accept that your bird will chew on any toy you buy, and that you will eventually have to replace it. When selecting toys for your cockatiel, keep a few safety tips in mind.

Size

Is the toy the right size for your bird? Large toys can be intimidating to small birds, which makes the birds less likely to play with them. On the other end of the spectrum, larger birds can easily destroy toys designed for smaller birds, and they can sometimes injure themselves severely in the process. Select toys that are designed for cockatiels and small parrots when choosing toys for your pet.

Safety

Is the toy safe? Good choices include sturdy wooden toys (either undyed or painted with bird-safe vegetable dye or food coloring) strung on closed-link chains or vegetable-tanned leather thongs, and rope toys. If you buy rope toys for your cockatiel, make sure her nails are trimmed regularly to prevent them from snagging in the rope, and discard the toy when it becomes frayed to prevent accidents.

Unsafe items to watch out for are brittle plastic toys that can easily be shattered into fragments by a cockatiel's busy beak, lead-weighted toys that can be cracked open to expose the dangerous lead to curious birds, loose link chains that can catch toenails or beaks, ring toys that are too small to climb through safely, and jingle-type bells that can trap toes, tongues, and beaks.

Cockatiel Favorites

Cockatiels enjoy the following types of toys: chewable wooden items, ranging from clothes pegs (not clothespins, which have springs that can snap on a bird's wing or leg) to thread spools; wooden ladders, sturdy ropes or cords to climb on; bells to ring; knotted rope or leather toys to preen and chew on; and mirrors to admire themselves in. Be warned, though, that if you give a single cockatiel a mirror toy, she may bond to the reflection she sees and consider the bird in the mirror a more interesting companion than you!

Cockatiels enjoy toys they can chew and bells they can ring.

Homemade Toys

As an alternative to store-bought toys, you can entertain your cockatiel with some everyday items you have around the house. Give your bird an empty paper towel roll or toilet paper tube (from unscented paper only, please) to chew. Let her shred subscription cards from your favorite magazines or chew up some clean computer paper. Give her a Ping-Pong ball to chase. String some Cheerios on a piece of vegetable-tanned leather or offer your bird a dish of raw pasta pieces to destroy.

When you're introducing new toys to your cockatiel for the first time, you might want to leave the toy next to the cage for a few days before actually putting it in the cage. Some birds accept new items in their cages almost immediately, but others need a few days to size up a new toy, dish, or perch before sharing cage space with it.

The Playgym

Although your cockatiel will spend quite a bit of time in her cage, she will also need time out of her cage to exercise and to enjoy a change of scenery. A playgym can help keep your pet physically and mentally active.

If you visit a large pet supply store or bird specialty store, or if you look through the pages of any pet bird hobbyist magazine, you will see a variety of playgyms on display. You can choose a complicated gym with a series of ladders, swings, perches, and toys, or you can purchase a simple T-stand that has a place for food and water bowls and a screw or two from which you can hang toys. If you're really handy with tools, you can even construct a gym to your cockatiel's specifications.

As with the cage, the location of your cockatiel's playgym will be an important consideration. You will want to place the gym in a secure location in your home that is safe from other curious pets, ceiling fans, open windows, and other household hazards. (Chapter 5 contains more information about making your home safe for your cockatiel.) You will also want the gym to be in a spot frequented by your family, so your bird will have company while she plays and supervision so she doesn't get into unsafe situations.

Chapter 5

Everyday Care

A cockatiel requires care every day to ensure his health and well-being. Birds are happiest when they are secure and comfortable in a safe environment. You can help your cockatiel feel more secure by establishing a daily routine and performing the same tasks at around the same time every day. This way, your cockatiel knows his needs will be met by the people he considers to be his family.

Here are some of the things you'll need to do every single day for your cockatiel:

- Observe your bird for any changes in his behavior or routine. Report any changes to your avian veterinarian immediately.
- Offer fresh food and remove old food. Wash the food dish thoroughly with detergent and water. Rinse thoroughly and allow the dish to air dry.
- Remove the water dish and replace it with a clean dish full of fresh water. Wash the soiled dish thoroughly with detergent and water.
- Change the paper in the cage tray.
- Let the bird out of his cage for supervised playtime.

Finally, you'll need to cover your bird's cage at about the same time every night to let him know it's bedtime. When you cover the cage, you'll probably hear your bird rustling around for a bit, perhaps getting a drink of water or a last mouthful of seeds before settling in for the night. Keep in mind that your cockatiel will require eight to ten hours of sleep a day, but you can expect that he will take naps during the day to supplement his nightly snooze.

Be Alert to Health Problems

Although it may seem a bit unpleasant to discuss, your bird's droppings require daily monitoring because they can tell you a lot about his general health. Cockatiels will produce tubular droppings that appear green in the center with a whitish edge. These droppings are usually composed of equal amounts of fecal material (the green edge), urine (the clear liquid portion), and urates (the white or cream-colored center). A healthy cockatiel generally eliminates between twenty-five and fifty times a day, although your bird may go more or less often.

You need to watch your bird carefully for changes that can indicate health problems. That includes noting changes in his behavior, and looking closely at his droppings every day.

Check the Dishes

Your bird should have clean water at all times, and this may mean refilling the water dish several times a day. Be sure to check your bird's seed dish daily, as well, to make sure he has seeds, rather than just empty seed hulls, in the dish. Refill the dish when necessary.

Texture and consistency, along with frequency or lack of droppings, can let you know how your pet is feeling. For instance, if a bird eats a lot of fruits and vegetables, his droppings are generally looser and more watery than a bird who primarily eats seeds. But watery droppings can also indicate illness, such as diabetes or kidney problems, which causes a bird to drink more water than usual.

The color of the droppings can also be an indication of health. Birds who have psittacosis typically have bright lime-green droppings, while healthy birds have avocado or darker green-and-white droppings. Birds with liver problems may produce droppings that are yellowish or reddish, while birds who have internal bleeding will produce dark, tarry droppings.

A color change doesn't necessarily indicate poor health. For instance,

Cleaning the Cage

Cage cleaning should be part of your weekly care routine. Here's how to do it.

- Remove your bird and all cage accessories before cleaning the cage.
- Wipe off (or scrape off) old food from the cage bars and the corners of the cage.
- Place the empty cage in the shower stall and turn on the shower. Running hot water over the cage helps loosen stuck-on food and other debris. Scrub the cage with a toothbrush or other stiff-bristled small brush to loosen anything that remains on the cage after it's been in the shower.
- Once all the debris has been removed, disinfect the cage with a bird-safe spray-on disinfectant that you can buy at a pet supply store. Let the disinfectant remain on the cage bars as directed by the instructions on the bottle, then rinse thoroughly to remove the disinfectant from the cage.
- Dry the cage completely. While the cage is drying, clean the perches and accessories. Scrape and wash the perches to keep them clean and free of debris. (Sand the perches with coarse-grain sandpaper from time to time to improve traction for your bird.) Replace perches that are very chewed or cannot be cleaned.
- Rotate the toys in the cage to keep your cockatiel's environment interesting. To protect your bird's health, discard toys that are broken, frayed, or worn.
- When the cage is completely dry, replace the accessories and put your bird back in his newly cleaned home.
- Clean the playgym the same way you cleaned the cage.

birds who eat pelleted diets tend to have darker droppings than their seed-eating companions, while parrots who have gorged on a particular fresh food soon have droppings with that characteristic color. Birds who overindulge on beets, for instance, produce bright red droppings that can look as though the bird has suffered some serious internal injury. Birds who overdo it on sweet potatoes, blueberries, or raspberries produce orange, blue, or red droppings. During pomegranate season, birds who enjoy this fruit develop violet droppings that can look alarming to an unprepared owner.

As part of your daily cage cleaning and observation of your feathered friend, look at his droppings carefully. Learn what is normal for your bird in terms of color, consistency, and frequency, and report any changes to your avian veterinarian promptly.

Seasonal Needs

Warm weather requires a little extra vigilance on your part to make sure your cockatiel remains comfortable. To help keep your pet cool, keep him out of direct sun, offer him lots of fresh, juicy vegetables and fruits (be sure to remove these fresh foods from the cage promptly to keep your bird from eating spoiled food), and mist him lightly with a clean spray bottle filled with plain water. Use this bottle only for misting your bird.

On a warm day, you may notice your bird sitting with his wings held away from his body, rolling his tongue, and holding his mouth open. This is how a bird cools himself off. Watch your bird carefully on warm days because he can overheat quickly and may suffer heatstroke, which requires veterinary care. If you live in a warm climate, ask your avian veterinarian how you can protect your bird from this potentially serious problem.

In the hot weather, your cockatiel will enjoy a cool mist.

Holiday Precautions

The holidays bring their own special set of stresses, and they can also be hazardous to your cockatiel. Drafts from frequently opening and closing doors can affect your bird's health, and the bustle of a steady stream of visitors can add to your pet's stress level (as well as your own).

Chewing on holiday plants, such as poinsettia, holly, and mistletoe, can make your bird sick, as can chewing on tinsel and ornaments. Round jingle-type bells can sometimes trap a curious bird's toe, beak, or tongue, so keep these holiday decorations out of your bird's reach. Watch your pet around strings of lights, too, as both the bulbs and the cords can be great temptations to curious beaks.

You must also pay attention to your cockatiel's needs when the weather turns cooler. You may want to use a heavier cage cover, especially if you lower the heat in your home at night, or move the bird's cage to another location in your home that is warmer and/or less drafty.

Household Hazards

The phrase "Curiosity killed the cat" could easily be rewritten as "Curiosity killed the cockatiel." These inquisitive little birds seem to be able to get into just about anything, which means they can get themselves into potentially dangerous situations rather quickly. Because of this natural curiosity, cockatiel owners must be extremely vigilant when their birds are out of their cage.

Part of this vigilance should include bird-proofing your home. Remember that some parrots are intellectually on a level similar to that of a toddler. You wouldn't let a toddler have free run of your house without taking precautions to safeguard the child from harm, and you should have the same concern for your cockatiel.

Let's go room by room and look at some of the potentially dangerous situations you should be aware of.

When your bird is out and about the house with you, take precautions to keep him safe.

Bathroom

This can be a cockatiel paradise if the bird is allowed to spend time with you as you prepare for work or for an evening out, but it can also be quite harmful to your bird's health. An open toilet could lead to drowning, the bird could hurt himself chewing on the electric cord of your blow-dryer, or he could be overcome by fumes from perfume, hairspray, or cleaning products, such as bleach, air freshener, and toilet bowl cleaner.

The bird could also become ill if he nibbles on prescription or nonprescription drugs in the medicine chest, or he could injure himself by flying into a mirror. Use caution when taking your bird into the bathroom, and make sure his wings are clipped to avoid flying accidents.

Kitchen

This is another popular spot for birds and their owners to hang out, especially around mealtimes. Here again, dangers lurk for curious cockatiels. An unsupervised bird could fly or fall into the trash can, or he could climb into the oven, dishwasher, freezer, or refrigerator and be forgotten. Your bird could land on a hot stove, or fall into an uncovered pot of boiling water or sizzling frying pan on the stove. The bird could also become poisoned by eating foods that are unsafe for him, such as chocolate, avocado, or rhubarb, if they are left unattended on a countertop.

Living Room

Are you sitting on your couch or in a comfortable chair as you read this book? Although it probably seems safe enough to you, your pet could be injured or killed if he decided to play hide-and-seek under pillows or cushions and you accidentally sat on him. Your cockatiel could become poisoned by nibbling on a leaded-glass lampshade, or he could fly out an open window or patio door. He could also fly into a closed window or door and injure himself severely. He could become entangled in a drapery cord or a venetian blind pull, he could fall into an uncovered fish tank and drown, or he could ingest poison by nibbling on ashes or cigarette butts in an ashtray.

Home Office

This can be another cockatiel playground, but you'll have to be on your toes to keep your pet from harming himself by nibbling on potentially poisonous markers, glue sticks or crayons, and electrical cords, or impaling himself on pushpins.

Other Areas of Concern

If you have a ceiling fan in your house, make sure it is turned off when your bird is out of his cage. Make sure you know where your bird is before turning on your washer or dryer, and don't close your basement freezer without checking first to be sure your bird isn't in there. Lit candles, inlaid jewelry, sliding glass doors, and toxic houseplants also pose threats to your cockatiel.

Assume your cockatiel will chew on every plant in your home, and get rid of all the toxic ones.

This doesn't mean you should keep your bird locked up in his cage all the time. On the contrary, all parrots need time out of their cage to maintain physical and mental health. The key is to be aware of some of the dangers that may exist in your home and to pay attention to your bird's behavior so you can intervene before the bird becomes ill or injured.

Nasty Fumes

Unfortunately, potential dangers to a pet bird don't stop with the furniture and accessories. A variety of fumes can overpower your cockatiel, such as those from cigarettes, air fresheners, insecticides, bleach, shoe polish, oven cleaners, kerosene, lighter fluid, glues, active self-cleaning ovens, hairspray, overheated nonstick cookware, paint thinner, bathroom cleaners, and nail polish remover. Try to keep your pet away from anything that has a strong chemical odor, and be sure to apply makeup and hair-care products far away from your cockatiel.

To help protect your pet from harmful chemical fumes, consider using some "green" cleaning alternatives, such as baking soda and vinegar to clear clogged drains, baking soda instead of scouring powder to clean tubs and sinks, lemon juice and mineral oil to polish furniture, and white vinegar and water as a window cleaner. These products keep the environment a little friendlier for your bird, and these simple solutions to cleaning problems often work better than higher-priced, name-brand products.

Nonstick Cookware

Marathon cooking sessions may result in overheated cookware or stovetop drip pans, which could kill your bird if the cookware or drip pans are coated with a nonstick finish. As it burns, toxic fumes are released that can kill a beloved pet bird. You may want to consider replacing your nonstick cookware with stainless steel pots and pans, which you can treat with a nonstick cooking spray to make cleanups safe and easy. By the same token, the self-cleaning cycle on some ovens can create harmful fumes for pet birds. Use this cycle only if you have opened the windows around your bird's cage to let in fresh air. (Make sure your cockatiel's cage is closed securely before opening a window.)

Home Improvements

If you're considering a remodeling or home improvement project, think about your cockatiel first. Fumes from paint or formaldehyde, which can be found in carpet backing, paneling, and particle board, can cause pets and people to become ill. If you are having work done on your home, consider boarding your cockatiel at your avian veterinarian's office or at the home of a bird-loving friend or relative until the project is complete and the house is aired out. You can consider the house safe for your pet when you cannot smell any trace of any of the products used in the remodeling.

Fumes from household cleaners can overpower your cockatiel. Consider using alternative cleaners such as baking soda and vinegar.

Pest Control

Having your home fumigated for termites poses another potentially hazardous situation for your pet cockatiel. Ask your exterminator for information about the types of chemicals that will be used in your home, and inquire if pet-safe alternatives, such as electrical currents or liquid nitrogen, are available. If your house must be treated chemically, arrange to board your bird at your avian veterinarian's office or with a friend before, during, and after the fumigation to ensure that no harm comes to your bird. Make sure your house is aired out completely before bringing your bird home, too.

Other Pets

Other pets can be harmful to your cockatiel's health, too. A curious cat could claw or bite your bird, a dog could step on him accidentally or bite him, or another, larger bird could break his leg or rip off his upper mandible with his beak. If your cockatiel tangles with another pet in your home, contact your avian veterinarian immediately because emergency treatment may be required to save your cockatiel's life.

Chapter 6

Feeding Your Cockatiel

Wild cockatiels spend a great deal of their time foraging for ripening grass sprouts, which are higher in carbohydrates and lower in proteins and fats than seeds alone. This need for sprouted fresh foods makes a simple seed-and-water diet unsuitable for pet birds. Poor diet also causes a number of health problems, including respiratory infections, poor feather condition, flaky skin, and reproductive problems, and is one of the main reasons some cockatiels live fairly short lives.

Along with providing nutrition for your cockatiel, food can serve as a mental diversion. Like their larger cousins the cockatoos, a cockatiel's nimble brain needs challenges throughout the day to keep her from becoming bored. If you hang a piece of fruit or vegetable from a hook in the center of the cage so your bird has to work to eat it, she'll enjoy the exercise!

Nutrition Requirements

According to avian veterinarian Gary Gallerstein, birds require vitamins A, D, E, K, B1, B2, niacin, B6, B12, pantothenic acid, biotin, folic acid, and choline to stay healthy, but they can only partially manufacture vitamin D3 and niacin in their bodies. A balanced diet can help provide the rest.

Along with the nutrients just listed, pet birds need trace amounts of some minerals to maintain good health. These minerals are calcium, phosphorus, sodium, chlorine, potassium, magnesium, iron, zinc, copper, sulphur, iodine, and manganese. These can be provided with a well-balanced diet and a supplemental mineral block or cuttlebone.

Ideally, your cockatiel's diet should contain about equal parts of seeds, grains, and legumes, and dark green or dark orange vegetables and fruits. You can supplement these with small amounts of well-cooked meat or eggs, or dairy products. Let's look at each part of this diet in a little more detail.

Seeds, Grains, and Legumes

The seeds, grains, and legumes portion of your bird's diet can include clean, fresh seed from your local pet supply store. Try to buy your birdseed from a store where stock turns over quickly. The dusty box on the bottom shelf of a store with little traffic isn't as nutritious for your pet as a bulk purchase of seeds from a freshly filled bin in a busy shop. When you bring the seeds home, refrigerate them to keep them from becoming infested with bugs.

To ensure your bird is receiving the proper nutrients from her diet, you need to know if the seed you're serving is fresh. One way to do this is to try sprouting some of the seeds. Sprouted seeds can also tempt a finicky eater to broaden her diet.

To sprout seeds, soak them overnight in lukewarm water. Drain the water off and let the seeds sit in a closed cupboard or other out-of-the-way place for twenty-four hours. Rinse the sprouted seeds thoroughly before offering them to your bird. If the seeds don't sprout, they aren't fresh and you'll need to find another source for your bird's food.

Be sure, too, that your pet has an adequate supply of seeds in her dish at all times. Some cockatiels are such neat eaters that they drop the empty seed hulls back into their dishes. This seemingly full dish can lead to a very hungry cockatiel if you aren't observant enough to check the dish carefully. Rather than just looking in the dish while it's in the cage, I suggest that you take the dish out and inspect it over the trash can so you can empty the seed hulls and refill the dish easily.

The seeds you feed your bird should be fresh and clean. But remember that birds cannot live on seeds alone.

Fresh Sprouts

Serving sprouts is a simple and nutritious way to expand your cockatiel's diet. Sprouted seeds are packed with vitamins and are a tasty addition to her diet. All you need is a sprouting jar, some mesh cloth, and a variety of seeds such as sunflower, mung, and radish. A health food store should carry this equipment, as well as instructions for sprouting seeds.

The first step is to wash and soak the seeds. The seeds should then be kept in a warm location to encourage sprouting. It is important that all of the material used is washed well to avoid spoiling. It takes about two to three days for the seeds to sprout. Once they have sprouted, offer them to your cockatiel for a nutritious treat. Refrigerate the leftovers, and don't keep them for more than a day or two.

One foodstuff that is very popular with cockatiels is millet, especially millet sprays. These golden sprays are part treat and part toy. Offer your cockatiel this treat sparingly, however, because it is high in fat and can make your cockatiel pudgy!

Other items in the bread group that you can offer your pet include unsweetened breakfast cereals, whole-wheat bread, cooked beans, cooked rice, and pasta. Offer a few flakes of cereal at a time, and serve small bread cubes and cockatiel-sized portions of rice, beans, or pasta.

Fruits and Vegetables

Dark green or dark orange vegetables and fruits contain vitamin A, which is an important part of a bird's diet and which is missing from seeds, grains, and legumes. This vitamin helps fight off infection and keeps a bird's eyes, mouth, and respiratory system healthy. Some vitamin A-rich foods are carrots, sweet potatoes, broccoli, dried red peppers, yams, dandelion greens, and spinach.

You may be wondering whether to offer frozen or canned vegetables and fruits to your bird. Some birds will eat frozen vegetables and fruits, while others turn their beaks up at the somewhat mushy texture of these defrosted foodstuffs. The high sodium content in some canned foods may make them unhealthy for your cockatiel. Frozen and canned foods will serve your bird's needs in an emergency, but I would offer only fresh foods as a regular part of her diet.

Fresh foods, including vegetables, are an important part of your bird's diet. Broccoli, parsley, carrots, and grated sweet potato are all good choices.

Other Fresh Foods

Along with small portions of well-cooked meat, you can also offer your bird bits of tofu, water-packed tuna, fully cooked scrambled eggs, cottage cheese, unsweetened yogurt, or low-fat cheese. Don't overdo the dairy products, though, because a bird's digestive system lacks the enzyme lactase, which means she is unable to fully process dairy foods.

Introduce young cockatiels to healthy people food early so that they learn to appreciate a varied diet. Some adult birds cling tenaciously to seed-only diets, which aren't healthy for them in the long term. Offer adult birds fresh foods, too, in the hope that they may try something new.

Whatever healthy fresh foods you offer your pet, be sure to remove food from the cage promptly to prevent spoiling and to help keep your bird healthy. Ideally, you should change the food in your bird's cage every two to four hours (about every thirty minutes in warm weather), so a cockatiel should be all right with a tray of food to pick through in the

Opting for Organics

Some pet bird owners prefer to feed their birds organic produce to offer maximum nutrition without pesticides and other additives that could be harmful to a bird. Look for organic produce at your local grocery store or farmer's market. Some manufacturers offer organic bird food, so be sure to check the product label on your cockatiel's formulated diet or seed mix to see if it's organic.

Vital Vitamins and Minerals

The foundation for cockatiel health starts with a balanced diet that offers sufficient quantities of vitamins (A, D, E, K, B1, B2, niacin, B6, B12, panthothenic acid, biotin, folic acid, and choline) and minerals (calcium, phosphorus, sodium, chlorine, potassium, magnesium, iron, zinc, copper, sulpher, iodine, and manganese). A mineral block of cuttlebone will supplement a well-rounded diet.

morning, another to select from during the afternoon, and a third fresh salad to nibble on for dinner.

Supplements

You may be concerned about whether your bird is receiving adequate amounts of vitamins and minerals in her diet. If your cockatiel's diet is mostly seeds and fresh foods, you may want to sprinkle a good-quality vitamin-and-mineral powder onto the fresh foods, where it has the best chance of sticking to the food and being eaten. Vitamin-enriched seed diets may provide some supplementation, but some of them add the vitamins and minerals to the seed hull, which your pet will discard while she's eating. Avoid adding vitamin and mineral supplements to your bird's water dish, because they can act as a growth medium for bacteria. They may also cause the water to taste different, which may discourage your bird from drinking.

Birds on pelleted diets do not need vitamin-and-mineral supplements because these complex diets already contain all the nutrients your cockatiel needs.

Water

Along with providing fresh foodstuffs at least twice a day, you will need to provide your cockatiel with fresh, clean water twice a day to maintain her good health. One technique is to give fresh water in the morning with vegetables and fruit and to replace the morning water that evening when you remove the perishable foods and give your bird seeds or pellets. The water cups tend to build up a dirty film, so take care to wash and rinse them thoroughly.

Wash and rinse all your bird's dishes every day when you change her food and water.

Foods to Avoid

Now that we've looked at foods that are good for your bird, let's look briefly at those that aren't. Among those foods considered harmful to pet birds are alcohol, rhubarb, avocado (the skin and the area around the pit can be toxic), as well as highly salted, sweetened, and fatty foods.

You should especially avoid chocolate because it contains the chemical theobromine, which birds cannot digest as completely as people can. Chocolate can kill your cockatiel, so resist the temptation to share this snack with her.

You also want to avoid giving your bird seeds or pits from apples, apricots, cherries, peaches, pears, and plums, because they can be harmful.

Let common sense be your guide in choosing which foods can be offered to your bird: If it's healthy for you, it's probably okay to share. However, remember to reduce the size of the portion you offer to your bird—a smaller cockatiel-sized portion will be more appealing to your pet than a larger, human-sized portion.

While sharing healthy people food with your bird is completely acceptable, sharing something that you've already taken a bite out of is not. Human saliva has bacteria that are potentially toxic to birds, so please don't share partially eaten food with your pet. For your bird's health and your peace of mind, give your cockatiel her own portion or plate.

What About Grit?

As a new bird owner, you may hear a lot of talk about the importance of grit in your bird's diet. Birds use grit in their gizzard to grind their food, much as we use our teeth. Avian veterinarians and bird breeders do not agree on how much grit birds need and how often it should be offered to them. Some will tell you birds need grit regularly, while others will advise against it.

If your cockatiel's breeder and your avian veterinarian think your bird needs grit, offer it sparingly (only about a pinch every few weeks). Do not offer it daily and do not provide your cockatiel with a separate dish of grit, because some birds will overeat the grit and suffer dangerous crop impactions as a result.

For the same reason, please don't kiss your cockatiel on the beak (kiss her on top of her little head instead) or allow your bird to put her head into your mouth, nibble on your lips, or preen your teeth. Although you may see birds doing this on television or in magazine pictures, it's really unsafe for your bird's health and well-being.

The Pelleted Diet Option

Cockatiels have played an important role in the creation of pelleted, or formulated, diets for all pet birds. In the early 1980s, researchers at the University of California, Davis, began conducting nutritional research on cockatiels to determine the best diet for pet birds. To be able to make precise comparisons of the different nutrients, the researchers created formulated diets for the test flock. Avian nutritionists have used the data gleaned from this test flock in creating many of the pelleted diets that are available today.

Pelleted diets are created by mixing as many as forty different nutrients into a mash and then forcing (or extruding) the hot mixture through a machine to form various shapes. Some pelleted diets have colors and flavors added, while others are fairly

TIP

Ingredients for a Healthy Cockatiel Diet

Seed mix
Pellets
Fresh vegetables
Fruits in smaller amounts
Vitamin supplements
Occasional treats

plain. These formulated diets provide more balanced nutrition in an easy-to-serve form that reduces the amount of wasted food and eliminates the chance for a bird to pick through a smorgasbord of healthy foods to find her favorites and reject the foods she isn't particularly fond of.

Starting a Pelleted Diet

Some cockatiels accept pelleted diets quickly, while others require some persuading. To convert your pet to a pelleted diet, offer pellets alongside of or mixed in with her current diet. Once you see that your bird is eating the pellets, gradually increase the amount of pellets you offer at mealtime while decreasing the amount of other food you serve. Within a couple of weeks, your bird should be eating her pellets with gusto!

If your cockatiel seems a bit finicky about trying pellets, another bird in the house may show your cockatiel how yummy pellets can be, or you may have to pretend that you are enjoying the pellets as a snack in front of your pet. Really play up your apparent enjoyment of this new food because it will pique your bird's curiosity and make the pellets exceedingly interesting.

Whatever you do, don't starve your bird into trying a new food. Offer new foods along with familiar favorites. This will ensure that your bird is eating and will also encourage her to try new foods. Don't be discouraged if your cockatiel doesn't dive right in to a new food. Be patient, keep offering new foods to your bird, and praise her enthusiastically when she samples something new!

It's okay to offer your bird a treat now and then. Just use your common sense when you choose treat foods, and make sure the majority of your bird's diet comes from the most nutritious foods.

Chapter 7

Grooming Your Cockatiel

Your cockatiel must be able to bathe regularly. He can do this himself—you just need to provide him with a suitable bath. There are also two grooming duties he cannot do himself—trimming his nails and his flight feathers to ensure his safety—and you will periodically have do them for him.

Although some people would say that a cockatiel's beak also needs trimming, I would argue that a healthy bird who has enough chew toys does a remarkable job of keeping his beak trimmed. If your bird's beak becomes overgrown, though, please consult your avian veterinarian. A parrot's beak contains a surprising number of blood vessels, so beak trimming is best left to the experts. Also, a suddenly overgrown beak may indicate that your bird is suffering from liver damage, a virus, or scaly mites, all of which require veterinary care.

Bathing

You can bathe your bird in a variety of ways: mist him lightly with a clean spray bottle filled with plain warm water, allow him to bathe in the kitchen or bathroom sink under a slow stream of water, or take him into the shower with you. Bathing is important to birds to help them keep their feathers clean and healthy, so don't deny your pet the chance to bathe at least once or twice a week.

Unless your cockatiel has gotten himself into oil, paint, wax, or some other substance that elbow grease alone won't remove and that could harm his feathers, he will not require soap as part of his bath. Under routine conditions, soaps and detergents can damage a bird's feathers by removing beneficial oils, so hold off on the shampoo during your cockatiel's normal bath.

Regular baths are an important part of bird care.

Let your bird bathe early in the day so his feathers can dry completely before bedtime. In cooler weather, you may want to help the process along by drying your pet off with a blow-dryer to prevent him from becoming chilled. To do this, set the blow-dryer on low and keep it moving so that your bird doesn't become overheated. He may soon learn that drying off is the most enjoyable part of his bath!

Nail Care

Cockatiels and other parrots need to have their nails clipped occasionally to prevent the nails from catching on toys or perches and injuring the bird. Lutino cockatiels have light-colored nails, which make it easier for owners to see where the nail stops and the blood and nerve supply (or quick) begins. In lutinos, the quick is generally seen as a pink line of color inside the nail. If your cockatiel has dark nails, you'll have to pare down the bird's nails carefully to make sure you do not cut the quick.

You will need to remove only tiny portions of the nail to keep your cockatiel's claws trimmed. Generally, a good guideline to follow is to remove only the hook on each nail, and to do this in the smallest increments possible. Stop well before you reach the quick. If you do happen to cut the nail short enough to make it bleed, apply a dab of cornstarch, followed by direct pressure, to stop the bleeding.

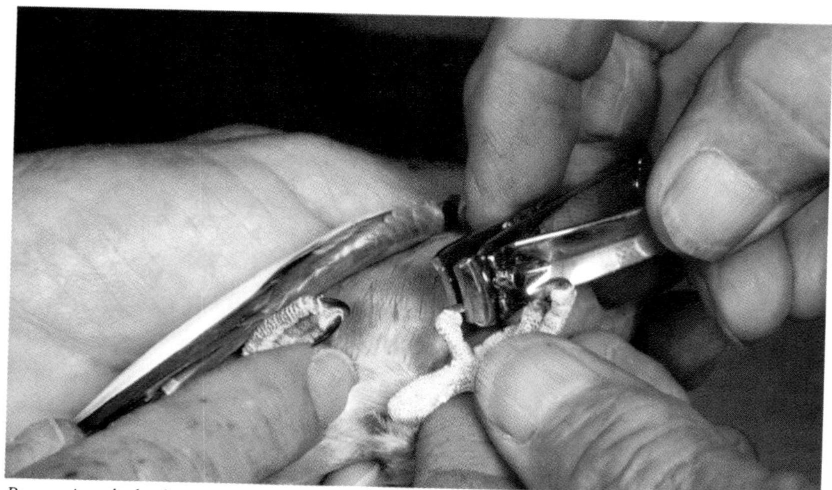
Remove just the hook part of each nail.

Wing Trimming

Cockatiels are among the fastest flying pet birds. Their sleek, slender bodies give them an advantage over larger birds, such as Amazons and African greys. Since cockatiels are so aerodynamic, you must pay close attention to the condition of the bird's wing feathers and trim them regularly to keep your bird safe. The goal of a proper wing trim is to prevent your pet from flying away or into a window, mirror, or wall while he's out of his cage. An added benefit of trimming your pet's wings is that his inability to fly well will make him more dependent on you for transportation, which should make him easier to handle. However, the bird still needs enough wing feathers so that if he is startled and takes flight from his cage top or playgym, he can glide safely to the ground.

Because this is a delicate balance, you may want to enlist the help of your avian veterinarian, at least the first time. Wing trimming is a task that must be performed carefully to avoid injuring your pet, so take your time if you're doing it yourself. Please do not just pick up the largest pair of kitchen shears you own and start snipping away, as this can cause severe injury to the bird's wingtips.

Feather Care Followup

Although it may seem as if your cockatiel's tail feathers need regular trimming, they don't under normal circumstances. Some cockatiels may thrash their tail feathers in the course of their normal activities, and you may feel better about

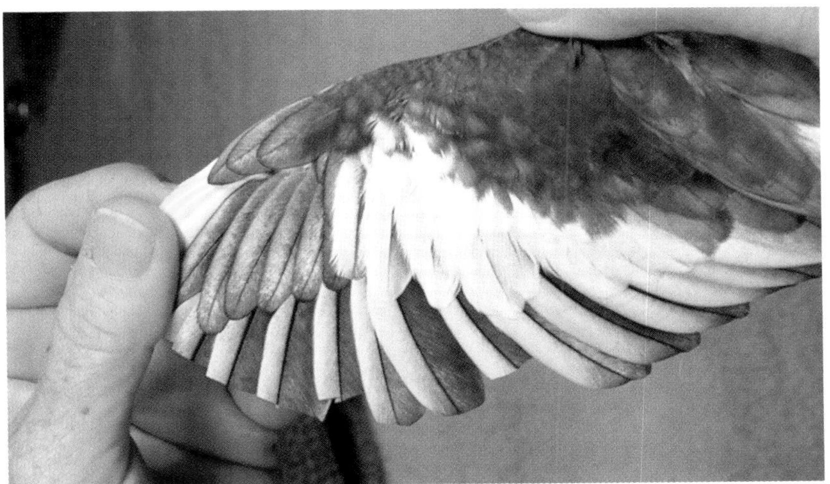

Trimming your bird's wings will help keep him safe at home. The outer flight feathers have been clipped here.

your bird's appearance if you trim the scruffy-looking feathers. However, if your bird's tail feathers are often damaged or ratty-looking, your cockatiel's cage may be too small for him to move about easily and comfortably. Remember that your pet's cage should be spacious enough for him to move around easily, extend his wings fully, and not have his crest touch the cage ceiling or the tip of his tail feathers touch the floor of the cage. If your bird's cage fails these simple tests, get a larger cage for your cockatiel and use the smaller cage as a travel cage or as a temporary home when you're cleaning the main cage.

Be particularly alert after a molt, because your bird will have a whole new crop of flight feathers that need attention. You'll be able to tell when your bird is due for a trim when he starts becoming bolder in his flying attempts. Right after a wing trim, a cockatiel generally tries to fly and finds he's unsuccessful at the attempt. He will keep trying, though, and may surprise you one day with a fairly good glide across his cage or off his playgym. If this happens, get the scissors and trim those wings immediately. If you don't, the section beginning on page 66 on finding lost birds may have more meaning for you.

Molting

At least once a year, your cockatiel will lose his feathers. Don't be alarmed, because this is a normal process called molting. Many pet birds seem to be in a perpetual molt, with feathers falling out and coming in throughout the summer.

Wing Trimming Step by Step

The first step in trimming your cockatiel's wing feathers is to assemble all the things you will need and find a quiet, well-lit place to groom your pet before you catch and trim him. Your grooming tools will include:

- Washcloth or small towel to wrap your cockatiel in
- Small, sharp scissors to do the actual trimming
- Needle-nosed pliers (to pull out any blood feathers you may cut accidentally)
- Flour or cornstarch (not styptic powder) to stop the bleeding in case a blood feather is cut
- Nail trimmers (while you have your bird wrapped in the towel, you might as well do his nails, too)

I encourage you to groom your pet in a quiet, well-lit place because grooming excites some birds and causes them to become wiggly. Having good light to work under will make your job easier, and having a quiet work area may calm your pet and make him easier to handle.

Once you've assembled your supplies and found a quiet grooming location, drape the towel over your hand and catch your cockatiel with your toweled hand. Gently grab your bird by the back of his head and neck (never compress the chest) and wrap him in the towel—firmly enough to hold him but not too tight! Hold your bird's head securely through the towel with your thumb and index finger. (Having the bird's head covered by the towel will calm him and will give him something to chew on while you clip his wings.)

Lay the bird on his back, being careful not to constrict or compress his chest (remember, birds have no diaphragm to help them breathe), and spread his wing out carefully. You will see an upper row of short feathers, called the covert feathers, and a lower row of long feathers, which are the flight feathers. Look for new flight feathers that are still growing in, also called blood feathers. These can be identified by their waxy, tight look (new feathers in their feather sheaths resemble the end of a shoelace) and their dark centers or quills—the dark color is caused by the blood supply to the new feather. *Never trim a blood feather.*

If your bird has a number of blood feathers, you may want to put off trimming his wings for a few days, because older, fully grown feathers act as a cushion to protect those just coming in from life's hard knocks. If your bird has only one or two blood feathers, you can trim the full-grown feathers accordingly.

To trim your bird's feathers, separate each one away from the other flight feathers and cut it individually (remember, the goal is to have a well-trimmed bird who is still able to glide a bit if he needs to). Start from the tip of the wing when you trim, and clip just five to eight feathers in. Use the primary covert feathers (the set of feathers above the primary flight feathers) as a guideline as to how short you should trim—trim the flight feathers so they are just a tiny bit longer than the coverts.

Be sure to trim an equal number of feathers from each wing. Although some people think that a bird needs only one trimmed wing, this is incorrect and could actually harm a bird who tries to fly with one trimmed and one untrimmed wing. Think of how off balance that would make you feel; your cockatiel is no different.

Now that you've successfully trimmed your bird's wing feathers, congratulate yourself. You've just taken a great step toward keeping your cockatiel safe. Now you must remember to check your cockatiel's wing feathers and retrim them periodically (about four times a year is a minimum).

Blood feather first aid

If you do happen to cut a blood feather, remain calm. You must remove it and stop the bleeding to ensure that your bird doesn't bleed to death, and panicking will do neither of you any good.

To remove a blood feather, use a pair of needle-nosed pliers to grasp the broken feather's shaft as close to the skin of the wing as you can. With one steady motion, pull the feather out completely. After you've removed the feather, put a pinch of flour or cornstarch on the feather follicle (the spot you pulled the feather out of) and apply direct pressure for a few minutes until the bleeding stops. If the bleeding doesn't stop after a few minutes of direct pressure, or if you can't remove the feather shaft, contact your avian veterinarian immediately for further instructions.

Although it may seem like you're hurting your cockatiel by removing the broken blood feather, consider this: A broken blood feather is like an open faucet. If left in, the faucet stays open and lets the blood out. Once removed, the bird's skin generally closes up behind the feather shaft and shuts off the faucet.

This molting cockatiel looks a little scruffy as his new feathers come in.

You can consider your bird in molting season when you see a lot of whole feathers in the bottom of the cage and you notice that he seems to have broken out in a rash of stubby little aglets (they look like those plastic tips on the ends of your shoelaces). Aglets are the feather sheaths that help new pinfeathers break through the skin, and they are made of keratin (the same material that makes up our fingernails). The sheaths also help protect growing feathers from damage until the feather completes its growth cycle.

You may notice that your cockatiel is a little more irritable during the molt. This is to be expected. Think about how you would feel if you had all these itchy new feathers coming in all of a sudden. However, your bird may actively seek out more time with you during the molt because owners are handy to have around when a cockatiel has an itch on the top of his head that he can't quite scratch! (Scratch these new feathers gently because some of them may still be growing in and may be sensitive to the touch.) Some birds may benefit from special conditioning foods during the molt; check with your avian veterinarian to see if your bird is a candidate for these foods.

TIP

Comfort During Molting

Encourage balanced nutrition.

Decrease stress by emphasizing security and rest periods.

Keep the room temperature between 75° and 80° during heavy shedding.

Promote preening activity.

If Your Bird Escapes

Now that we have covered wing trimming, it's as good a time as any to discuss the possibility of your bird escaping. One of the most common accidents that befalls bird owners is that a fully flighted bird (one with untrimmed wings) escapes through

Keeping Your Bird Safe

How can you prevent your bird from becoming lost? Here are some tips:

- Make sure his wings are safely trimmed at regular intervals.
- Trim both wings evenly and remember to trim them after your bird has molted.
- Make sure your bird's cage door locks securely and that his cage tray cannot come lose if the cage is knocked over or dropped accidentally.
- Check your window screens to be sure they fit securely and are free from tears and holes.
- Keep all window screens and patio doors closed when your bird is at liberty.
- Never go outside with your bird on your shoulder.

an open door or window. Just because your bird has never flown before or shown any interest in leaving his home or even his cage doesn't mean that he can't fly or that he won't become disoriented once he's outside.

Why don't lost birds come home? Some fall victim to predators in the wild, while others join flocks of feral, or wild, parrots (Florida and California are particularly noted for these). Still other lost birds end up miles away from home because they fly wildly and frantically in any direction. And some people who find lost birds don't advertise that they've been found because the finders think that whoever was unlucky

Pet cockatiels are not meant to live in the wild. Keep your bird safe by keeping him indoors.

Are Mite Protectors Necessary?

While we're discussing grooming and feather care, I'd like to recommend that you do not purchase mite protectors that hang on a bird's cage or conditioning products that are applied directly to a bird's feathers. Well-cared-for cockatiels don't have mites and shouldn't be in danger of contracting them. (If your pet does have mites, veterinary care is the most effective way to treat them.) Also, the fumes from some of these products are quite strong and can be harmful to your pet's health.

Conditioners, anti-picking products, and other substances that are applied to your bird's feathers will serve one purpose: to get your bird to preen himself so thoroughly in an effort to remove the offending liquid that he could remove all his feathers in a particular area. If you want to encourage your bird to preen regularly and help condition his feathers, simply mist him regularly with clean, warm water or hold him under a gentle stream from a kitchen or bathroom faucet. Your bird will take care of the rest.

or uncaring enough to lose the bird in the first place doesn't deserve to have him back.

How to Catch an Escaped Bird

If, despite your best efforts, if your bird escapes, you must act quickly for the best chance of recovering your pet. Here are some things to keep in mind:

- If possible, keep the bird in sight. This will make chasing him easier.
- Make an audiotape of your bird's voice (so you're ready for just such an emergency) and play it outside on a portable tape recorder to lure your bird back home.
- Place your bird's cage in an area where he is likely to see it, such as on a deck or patio. Put lots of treats and food on the floor of the cage to tempt your pet back into his home.
- Use another caged bird to attract your cockatiel's attention.
- Alert your avian veterinarian's office that your bird has escaped. Also let the local humane society and other veterinary offices in your area know.
- Post fliers in your neighborhood describing your bird. Offer a reward and include your phone number.
- Don't give up hope.

Chapter 8

Keeping Your Cockatiel Healthy

In general, cockatiels have a hardy resistance to disease and are very healthy birds. They have a strong survival instinct, and even when ill, cockatiels will continue to act normally for long periods of time. But cockatiels, like all pets, can get sick or injured. Since birds can't describe how they are feeling, it is very important that you understand the basics of your pet's physiology as well as the signs of illness. With preventive measures, early detection, and good care, the odds for a successful recovery are great.

Avian Anatomy

Your cockatiel's body is essentially very similar to that of a mammal. Both have skin, bones, muscles, sensory organs, and respiratory, cardiovascular, digestive, and nervous systems, although the various systems work in slightly different ways.

Skin

Your bird's skin is difficult to see, since your cockatiel has so many feathers. If you part the feathers carefully, though, you can see thin, seemingly transparent skin and the muscles beneath it. Modified skin cells help make up your bird's beak, cere, claws, and the scales on her feet and legs.

Birds cannot perspire as mammals do because birds have no sweat glands, so they must have a way to cool themselves off. On a warm day, you may notice your bird sitting with her wings held away from her body, rolling her tongue,

Modified skin cells make up your bird's beak, cere, and claws.

and holding her mouth open. This is how a bird cools herself off. Watch your bird carefully on warm days because she can overheat quickly, and she may suffer from heatstroke, which requires veterinary care. If you live in a warm climate, ask your avian veterinarian how you can protect your bird from this serious problem.

Musculoskeletal System

Next, let's look at your bird's skeleton. Did you know that some bird bones are hollow? These are lighter, making flying easier, but it also means these bones are more susceptible to breakage. For this reason, you must always handle your bird carefully! Another adaptation for flight is that the bones of a bird's wing (which correspond to our arm and hand bones) are fused for greater strength.

Birds also have air sacs in some of their bones (these are called pneumatic bones) and in certain body cavities that help lighten the bird's body and also cool her more efficiently.

Parrots have ten neck vertebrae, compared to a human's seven. This makes a parrot's neck more mobile than a person's (a parrot can turn her head almost 180 degrees). This gives the parrot an advantage in spotting food and predators in the wild.

During breeding season, a female bird's bones become denser to enable her to store the calcium needed to create eggshells. A female's skeleton can weigh up to 20 percent more during breeding season than she does the rest of the year because of this calcium storage.

Respiratory System

Your bird's respiratory system is highly efficient and works in a markedly different way from yours. Here's how your bird breathes: Air enters the body through your bird's nares, then passes through her sinuses and into her throat. As it does, the air is filtered through the choana, which is a slit that can easily be seen in the roof of many birds' mouths. The choana also helps clean and warm the air before it goes further into the respiratory system.

After the air passes the choana, it flows through the larynx and trachea, past the syrinx, or voice box. Your bird doesn't have vocal cords like you do; rather, vibrations of the syrinx membrane are what enable birds to make sounds.

So far it sounds similar to the way we breathe, doesn't it? Well, here's where the differences get bigger. As the air continues its journey past the syrinx and into the bronchi, your bird's lungs don't expand and contract to bring the air in and push it out. This is partly due to the fact that birds don't have diaphragms, as people do. Instead, the bird's body wall expands and contracts, much like a fireplace bellows. This action brings air into the air sacs mentioned earlier as part of the skeleton. This bellows action also moves air in and out of the lungs.

Although a bird's respiratory system is extremely efficient at exchanging gases in the system, two complete breaths are required to do the same work that a single breath does in people and other mammals. This is why you may notice that your bird seems to be breathing quite quickly.

Nervous System

Your cockatiel's nervous system is very similar to your own. Both are made up of the brain, the spinal cord, and countless nerves throughout the body that transmit messages to and from the brain.

Cardiovascular System

Along with the respiratory system, your bird's cardiovascular system keeps oxygen and other nutrients moving throughout her body, although the circulatory path in your cockatiel differs from yours. In your cockatiel, blood flowing from the legs, reproductive system, and lower intestines passes through the kidneys on its way back to the general circulatory system.

Digestive System

Your bird's body needs fuel for energy. Birds' bodies are fueled by food, which is where your bird's digestive system comes in. The digestive system provides the fuel that maintains your bird's body temperature—which is higher than yours. (The first time I bird-sat for friends, I worried about their cockatoo's seemingly hot feet. But when another bird owner told me that birds have higher temperatures than people, I stopped worrying about the bird's warm feet.)

Your cockatiel's digestive system begins with her beak. The size and shape of a bird's beak depend on her food-gathering needs. Compare the sharp, pointed

Your bird's feet may seem warm, but don't worry. It's only because birds have a higher normal body temperature than humans.

beak of an eagle or the elongated bill of a hummingbird with the small, hooked beak of your cockatiel.

Because cockatiels primarily eat seeds and other plant materials, their beaks have developed into efficient little seed crackers. Look closely at the underside of your bird's upper beak, if you can. It has tiny ridges that help your cockatiel hold and crack seeds more easily.

A parrot's mouth works differently than a mammal's. Parrots don't have saliva to break down and move their food, as we do. After the food leaves your bird's mouth, it travels down the esophagus, where it is moistened.

The food then travels to the crop, where it is moistened further and is passed in small increments into the bird's gizzard. Between the crop and the gizzard, food passes through the proventriculus, where digestive juices are added. Once in the gizzard, the food is broken down into even smaller pieces. The food next travels to the small intestine, where nutrients are absorbed into the bloodstream. Anything that's left over travels through the large intestine to the cloaca, which is the common chamber that collects wastes before they leave the bird's body through the vent. The whole process from mouth to vent usually takes only a few hours, which is why you may notice that your bird leaves frequent, small droppings in her cage.

Along with the solid waste created by the digestive system, your cockatiel's kidneys create urine, which is transported through ureters to the cloaca for excretion. Unlike a mammal, a bird does not have a bladder or a urethra.

Feathers

Birds are the only animals that have feathers, and they serve several purposes. Feathers help birds fly, they keep birds warm, they attract the attention of potential mates, and they help scare away predators.

Checking the Cage Bottom

Cockatiel droppings resemble smaller versions of the piles of droppings that bigger birds produce, with one exception. Because cockatiels come from such a dry environment in the interior of Australia, their droppings are drier than those of other, larger parrots who come from tropical jungle regions.

Bird droppings consist of three parts:

- The feces, which are the darker, solid portion of the droppings
- The urine, which is the liquid part of the droppings
- The urates, which is the creamy white portion of the droppings seen around the feces

Although bird droppings are probably among the least-appealing aspects of owning a pet bird, they are also one of the most important. The size, shape, color, consistency, and frequency of your bird's droppings can indicate health or illness. Any change from your bird's normal elimination routine can also signal health or behavioral problems that may require a veterinary evaluation.

Make it a habit to look at your bird's droppings each day. Does she seem to be eliminating more or less than usual? Are the droppings wetter than normal? Have they changed color? If you notice something out of the ordinary, contact your avian veterinarian's office for an evaluation appointment to ensure your cockatiel remains in good health.

Did you know that your cockatiel has between 5,000 and 6,000 feathers on her body? These feathers grow from follicles that are arranged in rows known as pterylae. The unfeathered patches of bare skin on your bird's body are called apteria.

A feather is a remarkably designed creation. The base of the feather shaft, which fits into the bird's skin, is called the quill. It is light and hollow, but remarkably

Feather colors are determined by pigments in the outer layer and interior structure of each feather.

tough. The upper part of the feather shaft is called the rachis. From the rachis branch the barbs and barbules (smaller barbs) that make up most of the feather. The barbs and barbules have small hooks on them that enable the different parts of the feather to interlock like Velcro and form the feather's vane or web.

Feather colors are determined by combinations of pigment in the outer layer and in the interior structure of the feather. All parrot species start out in their "wild" color, which is the color their feathers are in their native surroundings. In captive situations, new and unusual colors, called mutations, can occur. In the wild, birds of a different color mutation may be more easily spotted by predators (and eaten before they have a chance to breed and pass that color along to their offspring), but in captivity they can be paired with other different-colored birds to create even more mutations. These color mutations are most often seen in cockatiels, parakeets, lovebirds, Quaker parrots, ring-necked parrots, and grass parrots.

Birds have several different types of feathers on their bodies. Contour feathers are the colorful outer feathers on the body and wings. Many birds have an undercoating of down feathers that helps keep them warm. Semiplume feathers are found on a bird's beak, nares (nostrils), and eyelids.

A bird's flight feathers can be classified into one of two types. Primary flight feathers are the large wing feathers that push a bird forward during flight. They are also the ones that need clipping, which we discussed in chapter 7. Secondary flight feathers, found on the inner wing, help support the bird in flight. Primary and secondary flight feathers can operate independently. The bird's tail feathers also assist in flight by acting as a brake and a rudder.

To keep their feathers in good condition, healthy birds spend a great deal of time fluffing and preening. You may see your cockatiel seeming to pick at the base of her tail on the top side. This is a normal behavior in which the bird removes oil from the preen gland and spreads it on her feathers. The oil helps prevent skin infections and waterproofs the feathers.

Sometimes pet birds will develop white lines or small holes on the large feathers of their wings and tails. These lines or holes are referred to as stress bars or stress lines, and result from the bird being under stress as the feathers were developing. If you notice stress bars on your bird's feathers, discuss them with your avian veterinarian. Be prepared to describe to the veterinarian anything new in your pet's routine, because parrots are creatures of habit and sometimes react negatively to changes in their surroundings, diet, or daily activities.

Avian Senses

Taste

Birds can taste, but in a limited way because they have fewer taste buds in their mouths than people do. Also, their taste buds are contained in the roofs of their mouths, not in the tongue, as ours are. Experts therefore think that, compared to mammals, a parrot's sense of taste is poorly developed.

Vision

Cockatiels have a well-developed sense of sight. Birds see detail and can discern colors. Be aware of this when selecting cage accessories for your pet, because some birds react to changes in the color of their food dishes. Some seem excited by a different color bowl, while others act fearful of the new item.

Because her eyes are on the sides of her head, your bird relies on monocular vision, which means each eye is used independently.

Because their eyes are located on the sides of their heads, most pet birds rely on monocular vision, which means they use each eye independent of the other. If a bird wants to study an object, you will see her tilt her head to one side and examine the object with just one eye. Birds aren't really able to move their eyes around very much, but they compensate for this by having highly mobile necks that enable them to turn their heads about 180 degrees.

You have probably noticed that your bird lacks eyelashes. In their place are small feathers called semiplumes that help keep dirt and dust out of the bird's eyeball.

Like cats and dogs, birds have a third eyelid called the nictitating membrane that you will sometimes see flick briefly across your cockatiel's eye. The purpose of this membrane is to keep the eyeball moist and clean. If you see your cockatiel's nictitating membrane for more than a brief second, contact your avian veterinarian for an evaluation.

Hearing

You may be wondering where your bird's ears are. Look carefully under the feathers behind and below each eye to find them. The ears are somewhat large holes in the sides of your bird's head. Cockatiels have about the same ability to distinguish sound waves and determine the location of the sound as people do, but birds seem to be less sensitive to higher and lower pitches than their owners.

Smell

How does your cockatiel's sense of smell compare to your own? Birds seem to have a poorly developed sense of smell because smells often dissipate quickly in the air (where flying birds spend the majority of their time).

Touch

The final sense we relate to, touch, is well-developed in parrots. Parrots use their feet and their mouths to touch their surroundings (young birds, particularly, seem to "mouth" everything they can get their beaks on), to play, and to determine what is safe to perch on or chew on or eat.

Along with their tactile uses, a parrot's feet also have an unusual design compared to other caged birds. Unlike a finch, for example, which has three toes pointing forward and one back, two of the cockatiel's toes point forward and two point backward in an arrangement called zygodactyl. This enables a parrot to climb up, down, and around trees easily. Some larger parrots also use their feet to hold food or to play with toys.

Cockatiel Health Care

With good care, a cockatiel can live about twenty years, and some live well into their late twenties or thirties. One good example of cockatiel longevity was aviculturist Marie Olssen's bird, Bobbi, who was hatched in 1950 and died in

1985. At the time of his death, Bobbi was almost thirty-five years old! Unfortunately, the average life span of these small parrots is often much shorter. One of the reasons cockatiels don't live longer is that some owners may be reluctant to take their pets to the veterinarian. Some people don't want to pay veterinary bills for such "inexpensive" birds.

Most cockatiel owners believe the value of their bird goes far beyond the price they paid for her.

Choosing an Avian Veterinarian

As a caring owner, you want your bird to have good care and the best chance to live a long, healthy life. To that end, you will need to find a veterinarian who understands the special medical needs of birds and one with whom you can establish a good working relationship. The best time to do this is when you first bring your cockatiel home from the breeder or pet store. If possible, arrange to visit your veterinarian's office on your way home from the breeder or store. This is particularly important if you have other birds at home, because you don't want to endanger the health of your existing flock or your new pet.

If you don't know an avian veterinarian in your area, ask the person from whom you bought your cockatiel where they take their birds. (Breeders and bird stores usually have avian veterinarians on whom they depend.) Talk to other bird owners you know and find out who they take their pets to, or call bird clubs in your area for referrals.

If you have no bird-owning friends or can't locate a bird club, your next best bet is the Yellow Pages. Read the advertisements for veterinarians carefully and try to find one who specializes in birds. Many veterinarians who have an interest in treating birds will join the Association of Avian Veterinarians and advertise themselves as members of this organization. Some veterinarians have taken and passed a special examination that entitles them to call themselves avian specialists.

Once you've received your recommendations or found likely candidates in the telephone book, start calling the veterinary offices. Ask the receptionist how many birds the doctor sees in a week or month, how much an office visit costs, and what payment options are available (cash, credit card, check, or time payments). You can also inquire if the doctor keeps birds as pets.

If you like the answers you receive from the receptionist, make an appointment for your cockatiel to be evaluated. (If you don't, of course, move on to the next name on your list.) Make a list of any questions you want to ask the doctor regarding your bird's diet, how often your bird's wings and nails should be clipped, how often you should bring the bird in for an examination, and anything else you feel you need to know.

Alternative Health Treatments

Homeopathic treatments, herbal remedies, and acupuncture have become commonplace alternative medical treatments for people today, but did you know they can also be used to treat pet birds? Veterinarians began investigating alternative health treatments for pets in the 1980s, and today pet bird owners may be able to choose such treatments for their birds.

Birds may be good candidates for alternative medical treatments because of their physical and emotional makeup. Their natures are well suited to a holistic approach, which takes into account the bird's whole environment and routine when evaluating her health or illness. A bird owner who practices a holistic approach to bird care will carefully evaluate their bird daily for signs of illness while feeding her a top-quality diet and ensuring that the bird has an interesting and varied routine each day. If something is out of the ordinary during the owner's daily evaluation, they contact an avian veterinarian for an appointment as soon as the change is noted, rather than waiting to see what might happen to the bird.

Look in the Yellow Pages for veterinarians in your area who include holistic or alternative treatments in their practice, and call the office to find out whether the doctor treats birds. If you don't have a holistic veterinarian in your area, discuss alternative treatment options with your avian veterinarian to see if they are an option for your cockatiel when she is ill or injured.

Plan to arrive a little early for your first appointment because you will be asked to fill out a patient information form. This form will ask you for your bird's name; her age and sex; the length of time you have owned her; your name, address, and telephone number; your preferred method of paying for veterinary services; how you heard about the veterinary office; and the name and address of a friend the veterinary office can contact in case of emergency. The form may also ask you to express your opinion on the amount of money you would spend on your pet in an emergency, because this can help the doctor know what kind of treatment to recommend in such instances.

Don't take your bird to the local veterinarian who only sees cats and dogs. Birds are very different animals, and they need to see an avian veterinarian.

What the Veterinarian May Ask You

Do not be afraid to ask your avian veterinarian questions. Avian vets have devoted a lot of time, energy, and effort to studying birds, so put this resource to use whenever you can.

You may also be asked a number of questions by the veterinarian. These may include:

- Why is the bird here today?
- What is the bird's normal activity level?
- How is the bird's appetite?
- What does the bird's normal diet consist of?
- Have you noticed a change in the bird's appearance lately?

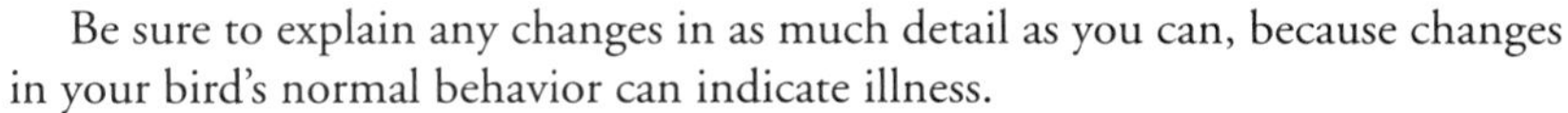

Be sure to explain any changes in as much detail as you can, because changes in your bird's normal behavior can indicate illness.

The Physical Exam

After the question-and-answer session with you, the exam will begin. To give the bird an opportunity to become accustomed to him or her, your veterinarian will probably take a first look at your cockatiel while she is still in her cage or carrier, rather than simply reaching right in and grabbing your pet. While the veterinarian is talking to you, he or she will check the bird's feather condition, her overall appearance, posture, and perching ability.

Next, the doctor will drape a towel over his or her hand and gently catch your cockatiel and remove her from her carrier or cage. When the bird is out of her carrier, the doctor will look her over carefully. He or she will note the condition of your pet's eyes, her beak, and her nares. The doctor will weigh your bird in a device that looks like a metal colander balanced on a scale, and the doctor will feel, or palpate, your bird's body, wings, legs, and feet for any abnormalities.

Once the examination is concluded and you've had a chance to discuss any questions you have with your veterinarian, the doctor will probably recommend a follow-up examination schedule for your pet. Most healthy birds visit the veterinarian annually, but some need to go more frequently.

Cockatiel Health Concerns

Although cockatiels are generally hardy birds, they are prone to a few health problems, including giardia, conjunctivitis, candida, roundworms, and papillomas. They, like all birds, can also suffer from respiratory problems and other conditions that result from a vitamin A deficiency, especially if they consume diets that are high in seeds and low in foods that are rich in vitamin A. Vitamin A deficiency can be prevented by feeding your bird a varied, healthy diet.

Giardia

Giardia is caused by a protozoan called *Giardia psittaci*. Signs of a giardia infection include loose droppings, weight loss, feather picking (especially under the wings), loss of appetite, and depression. Your avian veterinarian may have difficulty diagnosing this disease because the giardia organism is difficult to detect in a bird's feces. The disease can be spread through contaminated food or water, and birds are not immune to it once they've had it. Your veterinarian can recommend an appropriate medication to treat giardia.

In some birds, a giardia infection can lead to other problems, such as cockatiel paralysis syndrome, which is seen most often in lutino birds who are infected with *Giardia* or *Hexamita*. It's caused by a vitamin E and selenium deficiency. Signs include slow eye blink, weak jaw muscles, poor digestion, clumsiness, a weak grip, spraddle leg (a condition in which one or both of the bird's legs stick out sideways, leaving her unable to stand normally), weak hatchlings, an increase in the number of chicks who are dead in the shell, and decreased fertility. Antiprotozoal therapy and supplemental vitamin E and selenium have successfully treated the condition.

Conjunctivitis

Cockatiel conjunctivitis is seen in white or albino birds more than in normal grays. Signs include inflammation of the eyelid and discharge from the eye with no apparent cause. Treatment with topical antibiotic ointment temporarily resolves the signs, but recurrences are common. Affected birds should not be used in breeding programs because there is some evidence that this is a genetic problem.

If your bird's eyes don't look clear and bright, she needs to see her avian veterinarian.

Candida

Cockatiel breeders need to pay particular attention to candida, which is caused by the yeast *Candida albicans*. Young cockatiels seem to be particularly susceptible to candida infections, which occur when a bird's diet is low in vitamin A. Signs of candida include white, cheesy growths in the bird's mouth and throat, a loss of appetite, regurgitation or vomiting, and a crop that is slow to empty.

The trouble with trying to diagnose a candida infection is that many adult cockatiels don't show any signs of the condition, so a breeder may not even know he or she has infected birds until the parent birds pass the yeast to the chicks during feeding. Hand-fed chicks are not immune to the condition, either, because they can be affected by it if their throats are damaged by feeding tubes. Veterinary assistance in the form of antifungal drugs and a diet high in vitamin A may be your best weapons against candida.

Roundworms

Roundworms, or ascarids, can infest cockatiels who have access to dirt, which is where roundworm eggs are found. The worms themselves are two to five inches long and resemble white spaghetti. Mild infestations of roundworms can cause weight loss, loss of appetite, growth abnormalities, and diarrhea, while heavy infestations can result in bowel blockage and death.

To diagnose roundworms, your veterinarian will analyze a sample of your bird's droppings. He or she can then prescribe an appropriate course of treatment to clear up the problem.

Raccoon roundworms, which are passed in the animal's feces, can also affect cockatiels. To protect birds from this parasite, which can cause damage to a bird's central nervous system, prevent raccoons from getting access to your aviaries.

Sarcocystis

Another parasite problem, sarcocystis, can be a problem in North American areas with large opossum populations. Sarcocystis infections seem more prevalent in the winter months, and male birds are more susceptible to this parasite than females. Birds affected by sarcocystis often appear healthy one day and are dead the next. Those birds that do show signs of illness before dying become lethargic, cannot breathe easily, and pass yellowish droppings. As with the raccoon roundworms, preventing opossums from accessing your aviaries can eliminate the threat of this disease. However, cockroaches can also pass along this parasite by consuming opossum feces and then being eaten by an aviary cockatiel.

Papillomas

Papillomas are benign tumors that can appear almost anywhere on a bird's skin, including her foot, leg, eyelid, or preen gland. These tumors, which are caused by a virus, can appear as small, crusty lesions, or they may be raised growths that have a bumpy texture or small projections. If a bird has a papilloma on her cloaca, the bird may appear to have a wet raspberry coming out of her vent.

Many papillomas can be left untreated without harm to the bird, but some must be removed by an avian veterinarian because a bird may pick at the growth and cause it to bleed.

Bald Spots

Although this isn't really a health problem, some cockatiels, particularly lutinos, are prone to bald spots behind their crests. These bald spots resulted from inbreeding cockatiels to create the lutino mutation in the 1950s. Birds with noticeable bald spots on the backs of their heads are generally held out of breeding programs to try to keep the trait from being passed on to future generations.

Signs of Illness

To help your veterinarian and to protect your pet from long-term health problems, keep a close eye on her daily activities and appearance. If something suddenly changes in the way your bird looks or acts, contact your veterinarian immediately. Birds naturally hide signs of illness to protect themselves from predators, so by the time a bird looks or acts sick, she may already be dangerously ill.

Some signs of illness include:

- A fluffed-up appearance
- Loss of appetite
- Sleeping all the time
- A change in the appearance or number of droppings
- Weight loss
- Listlessness
- Drooping wings
- Lameness
- Partially eaten food stuck to the face or food has been regurgitated onto the cage floor
- Labored breathing, with or without tail bobbing
- Runny eyes or nose
- Stops talking or singing

If your bird shows any of these signs, please contact your veterinarian's office immediately.

Polyomavirus

Polyomavirus, which is sometimes called French moult, causes flight and tail feathers to develop improperly or not develop at all. Polyomavirus can be spread through contact with new infected birds, as well as from feather and fecal dust.

Adult birds can carry polyomavirus but not show any signs of the disease. These seemingly healthy birds can pass the virus to young birds who have never been exposed, and these young birds can die from polyomavirus rather quickly. Sick birds can become weak, lose their appetite, bleed beneath the skin, have enlarged abdomens, become paralyzed, regurgitate, and have diarrhea. Some birds with polyomavirus die suddenly.

Many avian health problems are highly contagious, which is why it's important to always quarantine a new member of the flock.

At present, there is no cure, although a vaccine is under development. Protecting your pets against polyomavirus and other diseases is why it's important to quarantine new birds and to take precautions, including showering and changing clothes, before handling your pet when you've gone to other bird owners' homes, to bird marts that have large numbers of birds from different vendors on display, and to bird specialty stores.

Psittacine Beak and Feather Disease Syndrome

Psittacine beak and feather disease syndrome (PBFDS) has been a hot topic among birdkeepers for the last decade. The virus was first detected in cockatoos and was originally thought to be a cockatoo-specific problem. It has since been determined that more than forty species of parrots, including cockatiels, can contract this disease, which causes a bird's feathers to become pinched or clubbed in appearance. Other symptoms include beak fractures and mouth ulcers. This highly contagious, fatal disease is most common in birds under three years of age, and there is no cure at present. A vaccine is under development at the University of Georgia.

Cockatiel First Aid

Sometimes your pet will get herself into a situation that will require quick thinking and even quicker action on your part to help save her from serious injury or death. Here are some basic first aid techniques that may prove useful in these situations. Before we get into the specific techniques, though, make sure you have your bird owner's first aid kit. (See the box on page 87 for information on what to include.)

Here are some urgent medical situations bird owners are likely to encounter, the reason they are medical emergencies, the signs and symptoms your bird might show, and what you should do for your bird.

Animal Bites

It's an emergency because: Infections can develop from bacteria on the biting animal's teeth and/or claws. Also, a bird's internal organs can be damaged by the bite.
Signs: Sometimes the bite marks can be seen, but often the bird shows few, if any, signs of injury.
What to do: Call your veterinarian's office and transport the bird there immediately. To save birds who have been bitten, veterinarians often treat for shock and prescribe antibiotics.

What to Do in an Emergency

If your bird requires urgent care, keep the following in mind:

Stay as calm as possible.
Stop any bleeding.
Keep the bird warm.
Keep the bird calm and quiet.
Call your veterinarian's office for additional instructions.
Describe what has happened to your bird.
Listen carefully to any instructions you receive.
Take your bird to the veterinarian's office or veterinary urgent care clinic as soon as possible.

A bird needs both her upper and lower beak to eat.

Beak Injury

It's an emergency because: A bird needs both her upper and lower beak (also called the upper and lower mandible) to eat and preen properly. Infections can also set in rather quickly if a beak is fractured or punctured.

Signs: The bird is bleeding from her beak. This often occurs after the bird flies into a windowpane or mirror, or if she has a run-in with a ceiling fan. The bird may have also cracked or damaged her beak, and portions of the beak may be missing.

What to do: Control the bleeding (see below), keep the bird calm and quiet, and contact your avian veterinarian's office.

Bleeding

It's an emergency because: A bird can withstand only about a 20 percent loss of blood volume and still recover from an injury.

Signs: With external bleeding, you will see blood on the bird, her cage, and her surroundings. In the case of internal bleeding, the bird may pass bloody droppings or bleed from her nose, mouth, or vent.

What to do: For external bleeding, apply direct pressure. If the bleeding doesn't stop with direct pressure, apply a coagulant, such as styptic powder (for nails and beaks) or cornstarch (for broken feathers and skin injuries). If the bleeding stops, observe the bird to check for more bleeding and signs of shock (see page 91). Call your veterinarian's office if the bird seems weak or if she has lost a lot of blood and arrange to take the bird in for further treatment.

Broken blood feathers can result in bleeding. Blood feathers can break horizontally (across the feather) or vertically (along the feather shaft). Horizontal breaks are more common, and they often result from a bird pulling at a blood feather or an owner accidentally cutting a blood feather while trimming a bird's wings.

In severe cases that do not respond to direct pressure, you may have to remove the feather shaft to stop the bleeding. To do this, grasp the feather shaft as close to the skin as you can with a pair of needle-nosed pliers and pull out the shaft with a swift, steady motion. Apply direct pressure to the skin after you remove the feather shaft.

Breathing Problems

It's an emergency because: Respiratory problems in pet birds can be life threatening.
Signs: The bird wheezes or clicks while breathing, bobs her tail, breathes with an open mouth, and has discharge from her nares or swelling around her eyes.
What to do: Keep the bird warm, place her in a bathroom with a hot shower running to help her breathe more easily, and call your veterinarian's office.

A healthy bird breathes with her mouth closed.

Burns

It's an emergency because: Birds who are burned severely enough can go into shock and may die.
Signs: A burned bird has reddened skin and burnt or greasy feathers. The bird may also show signs of shock (see page 91).
What to do: Mist the burned area with cool water. Lightly apply antibiotic cream or spray. Do not apply any oily or greasy substances, including butter. If the bird seems shocky or the burn is widespread, contact your veterinarian's office immediately for further instructions.

Concussion

It's an emergency because: A concussion results from a sharp blow to the head that can cause injury to the brain.
Signs: Birds sometimes suffer concussions when they fly into mirrors or windows. They will seem stunned and may go into shock.

What to do: Keep the bird warm, prevent her from hurting herself further, and watch her carefully. Alert your veterinarian's office to the injury.

Cloacal Prolapse

It's an emergency because: The bird's lower intestines, uterus, or cloaca is protruding from the bird's vent.
Signs: The bird has pink, red, brown, or black tissue protruding from her vent.
What to do: Contact your veterinarian's office for immediate care. Your veterinarian can usually reposition the organs.

Egg Binding

It's an emergency because: The egg blocks the hen's excretory system and makes it impossible for her to eliminate. Also, eggs can sometimes break inside the hen, which can lead to infection.
Signs: An egg-bound hen strains to lay eggs unsuccessfully. She becomes fluffed and lethargic, sits on the floor of her cage, may be paralyzed, and may have a swollen abdomen.

Females will lay eggs even if there are no males around.

Your Cockatiel's First Aid Kit

Assemble a bird owner's first aid kit so that you will have some basic supplies on hand before your bird needs them. Here's what to include:

- Appropriate-size towels for catching and holding your bird
- Heating pad, heat lamp, or other heat source
- Pad of paper and pencil to make notes about the bird's condition
- Styptic powder, silver nitrate stick, and cornstarch to stop bleeding (use styptic powder or silver nitrate stick on beak and nails only)
- Blunt-tipped scissors
- Nail clippers and nail file
- Needle-nosed pliers to pull broken blood feathers
- Blunt-end tweezers
- Hydrogen peroxide or other disinfectant solution
- Eye irrigation solution
- Bandage materials such as gauze squares, masking tape (it doesn't stick to a bird's feathers as adhesive tape does), and gauze rolls
- Pedialyte or other energy supplement
- Eye dropper
- Small syringes without the needles to irrigate wounds or to feed sick birds
- Penlight

What to do: Keep her warm, because this sometimes helps her pass the egg. Put her and her cage into a warm bathroom with a hot shower running to increase the humidity, which may also help her pass the egg. If your bird doesn't improve within an hour, contact your veterinarian.

Eye Injuries

It's an emergency because: Untreated eye problems may lead to blindness.
Signs: Swollen or pasty eyelids, discharge, cloudy eyeball, and increased rubbing of eye area.
What to do: Examine the eye carefully for foreign bodies. Then contact your veterinarian for instructions.

Fractures

It's an emergency because: A fracture can cause a bird to go into shock. Depending on the type of fracture, infections can also set in.
Signs: Birds most often break bones in their legs, so be on the lookout for a bird who is holding one leg at an odd angle or who isn't putting weight on one leg. Sudden swelling of a leg or wing, or a droopy wing can also indicate fractures.
What to do: Confine the bird to her cage or a small carrier. Don't handle her unnecessarily. Keep her warm and contact your veterinarian.

Frostbite

It's an emergency because: A bird could lose toes or feet to frostbite. She could also go into shock and die.
Signs: The frostbitten area is very cold and dry to the touch and is pale in color.
What to do: Warm up the damaged tissue gradually in a circulating warm (not hot) water bath. Keep the bird warm and contact your veterinarian's office for further instructions.

Inhaled or Eaten Foreign Object

It's an emergency because: Birds can develop serious respiratory or digestive problems from foreign objects in their bodies.
Signs: In the case of inhaled items, symptoms include wheezing and other respiratory problems. In the case of consumed objects, you may have seen the bird playing with a small item that suddenly cannot be found.
What to do: If you suspect that your bird has inhaled or eaten something she shouldn't have, contact your veterinarian's office immediately.

Cockatiels, like all parrots, like to chew on everything. Sometimes that can get them into trouble.

Lead Poisoning

It's an emergency because: Birds can die from lead poisoning.
Signs: A bird with lead poisoning may act depressed or weak. She may be blind, or she may walk in circles at the bottom of her cage. She may regurgitate or pass droppings that resemble tomato juice.

What to do: Contact your avian veterinarian immediately. Lead poisoning requires a quick start to treatment, and the treatment may require several days or weeks to complete successfully.

> **CAUTION**
>
> **Get the Lead Out**
>
> Lead poisoning is easily prevented by keeping birds away from common sources of lead in the home. These include stained-glass items, leaded paint found in some older homes, fishing weights, drapery weights, and some parrot toys (some are weighted with lead). One item that won't cause lead poisoning is a lead pencil (they're actually graphite).

Overheating

It's an emergency because: High body temperatures can kill a bird.
Signs: An overheated bird will try to make herself thin. She will hold her wings away from her body, open her mouth, and roll her tongue in an attempt to cool herself. Birds don't have sweat glands, so they must try to cool their bodies by exposing as much of their skin's surface as they can to moving air.
What to do: Cool the bird off by putting her in front of a fan (make sure the blades are screened so the bird doesn't injure herself further), by spraying her with cool water, or by having her stand in a bowl of cool water. Let the bird drink cool water if she can (if she can't, offer her cool water with an eyedropper) and contact your veterinarian.

Birds cool themselves by holding their wings away from their body.

Can You Catch Avian Flu from Your Bird?

Zoonotic diseases, or diseases that can be passed between animals and people, have gotten a great deal of attention in the first part of the twenty-first century, thanks to diseases such as avian flu, which came to public attention in late 2003 when outbreaks were reported in Asia. Ten countries reported outbreaks in 2004, and fifty-five people worldwide contracted the disease from birds. When this book went to press, the Centers for Disease Control and Prevention had a plan in place to combat avian flu in the event of an outbreak in the United States, and vaccines to combat the disease are under development.

Avian flu is an infectious disease that is caused by Type A strains of the influenza virus. It infects mostly waterfowl, such as ducks, and it can spread to domestic poultry. Wild birds worldwide may be carriers of avian flu. Carrier birds often do not show signs of illness, but they shed the virus through their droppings, nasal secretions, or saliva.

Avian flu is of particular concern to poultry farmers in the United States. Since 1997, about 16 outbreaks of avian flu have been reported

Poisoning

It's an emergency because: Poisons can kill a bird quickly.
Signs: Poisoned birds may suddenly regurgitate, have diarrhea or bloody droppings, and have redness or burns around their mouths. They may also go into convulsions, become paralyzed, or go into shock.
What to do: Put the poison out of your bird's reach. Contact your veterinarian for further instructions. Be prepared to take the poison with you to the vet's office in case he or she needs to contact a poison control center for further information.

Seizures

It's an emergency because: Seizures can indicate a number of serious conditions, including lead poisoning, infections, nutritional deficiency, heat stroke, and epilepsy.

on U.S. poultry farms. These outbreaks were classified as low pathogenic, which means few birds became ill or died. This is in direct contrast to the cases reported in Asia in 2003 and 2004, when thousands of birds became ill or were euthanized to stop the spread of the disease.

People can catch avian flu by coming in contact with the droppings of infected birds or with the birds themselves. This is what happened in Asia during the outbreaks in 2003 and 2004. Symptoms of avian flu in people can range from the typical flulike symptoms, such as fever, cough, sore throat, and muscle aches, to eye infection, pneumonia, and other life-threatening complications. Clinical signs in birds can vary, from birds who show no signs of illness to any of the following: lack of energy and appetite, decreased egg production, soft-shelled or misshapen eggs, nasal discharge, sneezing, a lack of coordination, and loose droppings.

Let me emphasize that it is extremely unlikely that your cockatiel is a carrier of avian flu or that you could catch avian flu from your pet. Avian flu is a greater concern for poultry farmers and bird breeders than it is for the average pet bird owner. I am including information here because the topic has received a lot of attention in television and newspaper reports.

Signs: The bird goes into a seizure that lasts from a few seconds to a minute. Afterward, she seems dazed and may stay on the cage floor for several hours. She may also appear unsteady and won't perch.

What to do: Keep the bird from hurting herself by removing everything you can from her cage. Cover the bird's cage with a towel and darken the room to reduce the bird's stress level. Contact your veterinarian's office immediately for further instructions.

Shock

It's an emergency because: Shock occurs when the bird's circulatory system cannot move the blood supply around the bird's body. This is a serious condition that can lead to death if left untreated.

Signs: Shocky birds may act depressed, breathe rapidly, and have a fluffed appearance. If your bird displays these signs in conjunction with a recent accident, suspect shock and take appropriate action.

What to do: Keep your bird warm, cover her cage, and transport her to your veterinarian's office as soon as possible.

Medicating Your Cockatiel

Most bird owners are faced with the prospect of medicating their pets at some point in the birds' lives, and many are not sure if they can complete the task without hurting their pets. If you have to medicate your pet, your avian veterinarian or veterinary technician should explain the process to you. In the course of the explanation, you should find out how you will be administering the medication, how much of the drug you will be giving your bird, how often the bird needs the medication, and how long the entire course of treatment will last.

If you find (as I often have) that you've forgotten one or more of these steps after you arrive home, call your vet's office for clarification to make sure your bird receives the follow-up care from you that she needs.

Let's briefly review the most common methods of administering medications to birds (which are discussed completely in *The Complete Bird Owner's Handbook* by Gary A. Gallerstein, DVM). I know from personal experience that all the methods I describe here do work and can be done with minimal stress to both bird and owner.

Your cockatiel relies on you to do what is best for her.

Oral Medication

This is a good route to take with birds who are small, easy to handle, or underweight. The medication is usually given with a plastic syringe, minus the needle, placed in the left side of the bird's mouth and pointed toward the right side of her throat. This route is recommended to ensure that the medication gets into the bird's digestive system and not into her lungs, where aspiration pneumonia can result.

Medicating a bird's food or offering medicated feed is another effective possibility, but medications added to a bird's water supply are often less effective because sick birds are less likely to drink water,

Convalescing Cockatiels

Veterinarian Michael Murray recommends that bird owners keep the following tips in mind when a birds is ill:

- **Keep the bird warm.** You can do this by putting the bird in an empty aquarium with a heating pad under her, by putting a heat lamp near the bird's cage, or by putting a heating pad set on low under the bird's cage in place of the cage tray. Whatever heat source you choose to use, make sure to keep a close eye on your bird so that she doesn't accidentally burn herself on the pad or lamp and doesn't chew on a power cord.
- **Put the bird in a dark, quiet room.** This helps reduce the bird's stress.
- **Put the bird's food in locations that are easy to reach.** Sick birds need to eat, but they may not be able to reach the food in its normal locations in the cage. Sometimes, birds require hand feeding to keep their calorie consumption steady.
- **Protect the bird from additional injury.** If the convalescing bird is in a clear-sided aquarium, for example, you may want to put a towel over the glass to keep the bird from flying into it.

and the medicated water may have an unusual taste that makes the bird less likely to drink it.

Injected Medication

Avian veterinarians consider this the most effective method of medicating birds. Some injection sites—into a vein, beneath the skin, or into a bone—are used by avian veterinarians in the clinic. Bird owners are usually asked to medicate their birds intramuscularly—by injecting medication into the bird's chest muscle. This is the area of the bird's body that has the greatest muscle mass, so it is a good injection site.

It's perfectly understandable if you're hesitant about giving your bird shots. I was apprehensive the first time I had to medicate a bird this way, but we both survived the procedure. Wrap your bird securely but comfortably in a washcloth or small towel and lay her on your lap with her chest up. Hold her head securely with your thumb and index finger of one hand, and use the other to insert the syringe at about a 45-degree angle under the bird's chest feathers and into the muscle beneath.

You should remember to alternate the side you inject your bird on (say, left in the morning and right in the evening) to ensure that one side doesn't get overinjected and sore. Remain calm and talk to your bird in a soothing tone while you're administering the drugs. Before you both know it, the shot is over and your bird is one step closer to a complete recovery!

Topical Medication

This method, which is far less stressful than injections, provides medication directly to a part of a bird's body. Uses can include medications for eye infections, dry skin on the feet or legs, and sinus problems.

Caring for Older Birds

If you've offered your cockatiel a varied, healthy diet, taken her to the vet regularly, clipped her wings faithfully, and kept her environment clean and interesting, chances are your bird will live into old age. You may notice subtle changes in your bird's appearance and habits as she ages. She may molt more erratically and her feathers may grow in more sparsely, or she may seem to preen herself less often.

Although little is known about the nutritional requirements of older pet birds, avian veterinarians Branson W. Ritchie and Greg J. Harrison suggest in their book *Avian Medicine: Principles and Applications* that older pet birds should eat a highly digestible diet that enables a bird to maintain her weight

Older birds may preen themselves less often.

while getting lower levels of proteins, phosphorus, and sodium. They also suggest that this diet contain slightly higher levels of vitamins A, E, B12, thiamin, pyridoxine, zinc, linoleic acid, and lysine to help birds cope with the metabolic and digestive changes that come with old age.

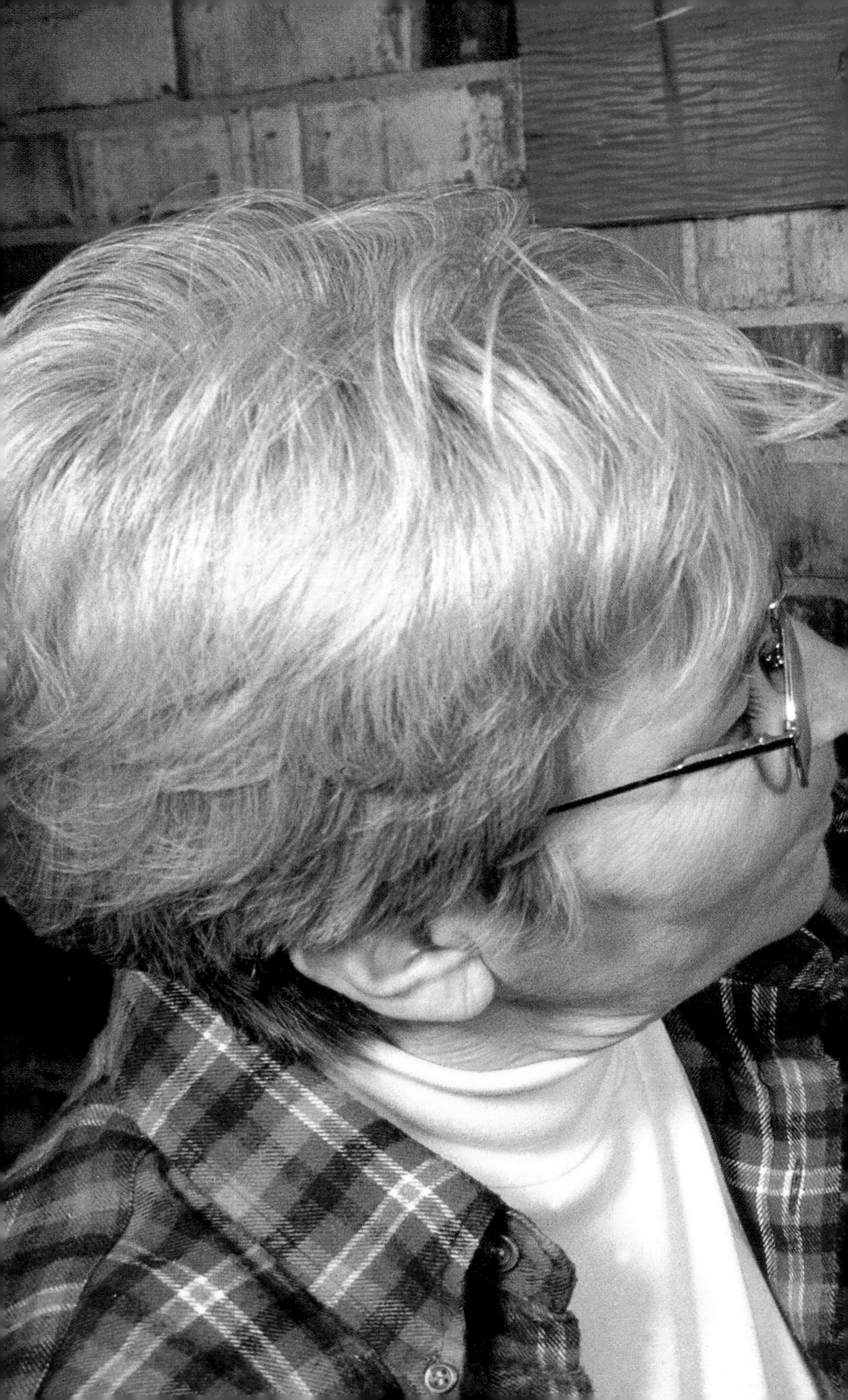

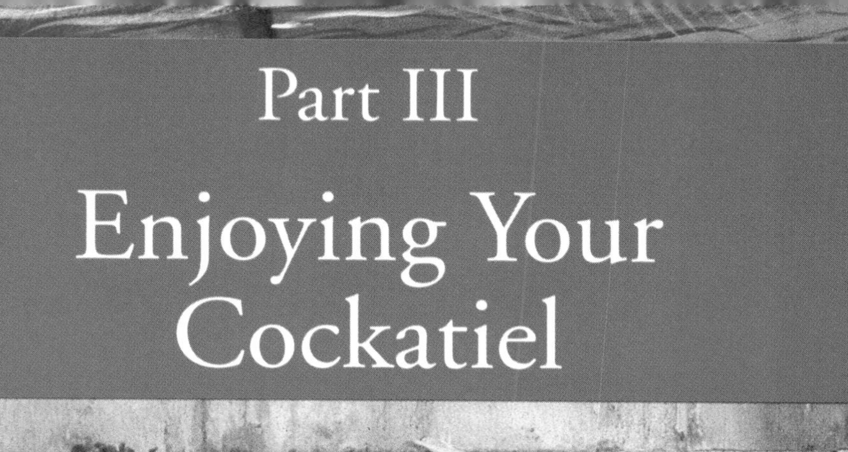

Part III

Enjoying Your Cockatiel

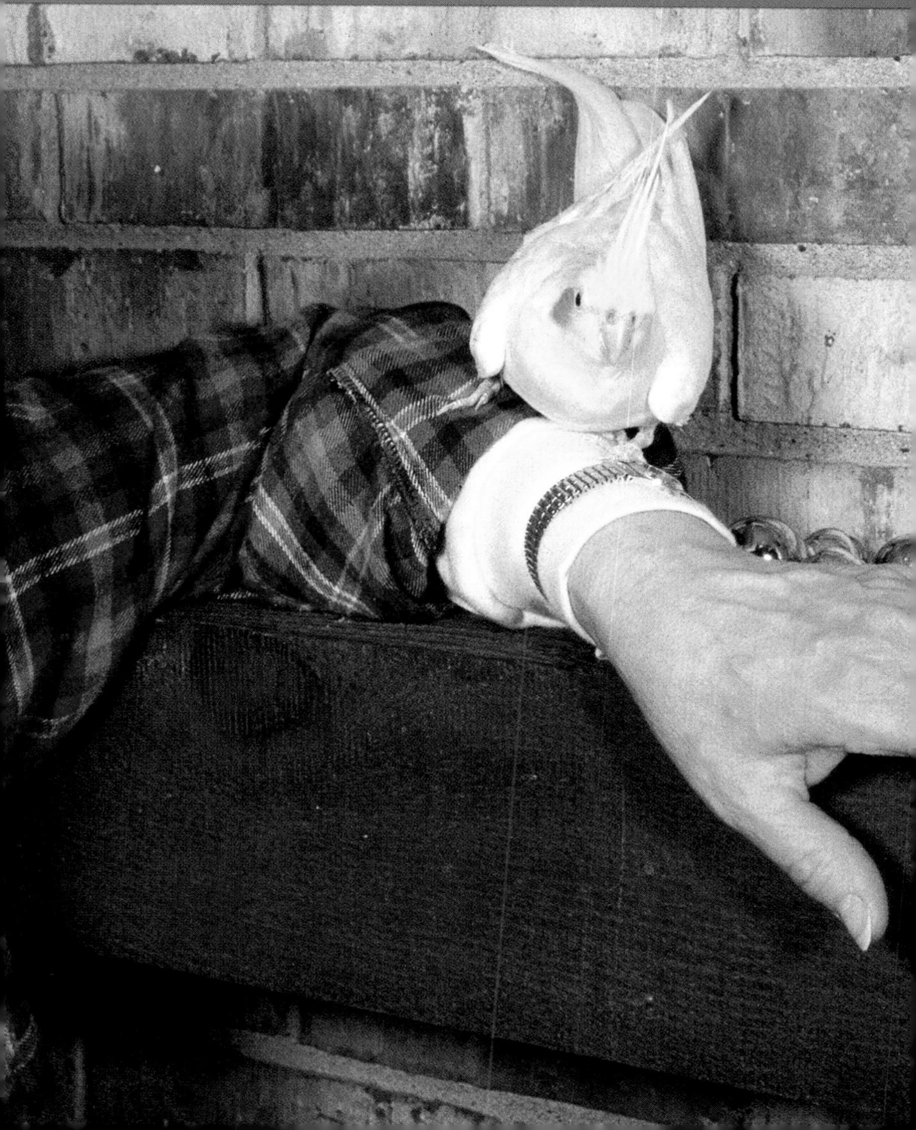

Chapter 9

Understanding Your Cockatiel

Most new bird owners have high expectations for developing a loving relationship with their pet. The goal is to nurture a relationship with your cockatiel that will result in a bird who will interact well with people, be pleasant company, and show few signs of aggressiveness (such as screaming). Sometimes, however, we forget that birds in captivity are not in their natural surroundings and can't always live up to our expectations. Knowing about, understanding, and respecting your cockatiel's natural behavior will help you both have a trusting and happy relationship.

Common Cockatiel Behaviors

The following common avian behaviors are listed in alphabetical order to help you better understand your new, feathered friend.

Attention Getting

As your cockatiel becomes more settled in your home, don't be surprised if you hear subtle little fluffs coming from under the cage cover first thing in the morning. It's as if your bird is saying "I hear that you're up. I'm up too! Don't forget to uncover my cage and play with me." Other attention-getting behaviors include gently shaking toys, sneezing, and soft vocalizations.

Beak Grinding

If you hear your bird making odd little grinding noises as he's drifting off to sleep, don't be alarmed. Beak grinding is a sign of a contented pet bird, and it's commonly heard as a bird settles in for the night.

Beak Wiping

After a meal, it's common for a cockatiel to wipe his beak against a perch or on the cage floor to clean it.

Birdie Aerobics

This is how I describe a sudden bout of stretching that all parrots seem prone to. An otherwise calm bird will suddenly grab the cage bars and stretch the wing and leg muscles on one side of his body, or he will raise both wings in imitation of an eagle.

Eye Pinning

This is what happens when your cockatiel sees something that excites him. His pupils will become large, then contract, then get large again. Birds will pin their eyes when they see a favorite food, a favored person, another bird, or a special toy. In larger parrots, this can also be a sign of confused emotions that can leave an owner vulnerable to a nasty bite. Your parakeet may also bite when he's in "emotional overload," so watch out!

When the pupils of your bird's eyes dilate and then contract, he is excited or delighted.

Feather Picking

Don't confuse this with preening (see page 101). Feather picking often results from physical problems, such as a dietary imbalance, a hormonal change, a thyroid problem, or an infection of the skin or feathers. Cockatiels who suddenly begin picking their feathers, especially the feather under the wings, may have an intestinal parasite called giardia.

It can also be caused by emotional upset, such as a change in the owner's appearance, a change in the bird's routine, another pet being added to the home, a new baby in the home, or a number of other stressors. Although it looks painful to us, some birds find the routine of pulling out their feathers emotionally soothing.

Once a bird starts feather picking, it may be difficult to get him to stop. If you notice that your bird suddenly starts pulling his feathers out, contact your avian veterinarian for an evaluation.

Fluffing can be a prelude to preening or a way to relieve stress.

Fluffing

This is often a prelude to preening or a tension releaser. If your bird fluffs up, stays fluffed, and resembles a little feathered pinecone, however, contact your avian veterinarian for an appointment because fluffed feathers can be a sign of illness.

Hissing

If your cockatiel hisses, it's because he's frightened of something in his environment and he's trying to scare it away by hissing.

Mutual Preening

This is part of the preening behavior described on page 101, and it can take place between birds or between birds and their owners. Mutual preening is a sign of affection reserved for best friends or mates, so consider it an honor if your cockatiel wants to preen your eyebrows, hair, mustache, or beard, or your arms and hands.

Napping

You will probably catch your cockatiel taking a little birdnap during the day. These active little birds seem to be either going full-tilt, playing and eating, or catching a few zzzz's. As long as you see no other indications of illness, such as a loss of appetite or a fluffed-up appearance, there is no need to worry if your pet sleeps during the day.

Pair Bonding

Mated pairs bond, but so do best bird buddies of the same sex. Buddy pairs will demonstrate some of the same behavior as mated pairs, including sitting close to each other, preening each other, and mimicking one another's actions, such as stretching or scratching, often at the same time.

Possessiveness

Cockatiels can become overly attached to one person in the household, especially if that person is the one who is primarily responsible for the bird's care. Indications of a possessive cockatiel can include hissing and other threatening gestures made toward other family members, and pair bonding behavior with the chosen family member. You can keep your cockatiel from becoming possessive by having all members of the family spend time with him from the time you first bring him home. Encourage different members of the family to feed the bird and clean his cage, and make sure all family members play with the bird and socialize with him while he's out of his cage.

Preening

This is part of a cockatiel's normal routine. You will see your bird ruffling and straightening his feathers each day. He will also take oil from the uropygial or preen gland at the base of his tail and put it on the rest of his feathers, so don't be concerned if you see your pet seeming to peck or bite at his tail. If, during molting, your bird seems to remove whole feathers, don't panic! Old, worn feathers are pushed out by incoming new ones, which make the old feathers loose and easy to remove.

Preening is part of your bird's daily routine. Lucky for birds that they are such contortionists!

Regurgitating

If you see that your bird is pinning his eyes, bobbing his head, and pumping his neck and crop muscles, he is about to regurgitate some food for you. Birds regurgitate to their mates during breeding season and to their young while raising

Learn to Read a Cockatiel's Crest

A cockatiel's crest will tell you a lot about his mood. Here's what to look for.

- Content cockatiels keep their crests lowered. Only the tips of the feathers point upward.
- Playful, alert cockatiels raise their crests vertically. This position indicates that the bird is ready for action.
- Agitated cockatiels raise their crests straight up, and the feathers' tips lean forward slightly.
- Frightened cockatiels whip their crests back and hiss in a threatening manner. They also stand tall, ready to fight or take flight, as the situation indicates.

chicks. It is a mark of great affection to have your bird regurgitate his dinner for you, so try not to be too disgusted if your pet starts bringing up his latest meal.

Birds only scream when they're not getting the love and attention they crave.

Resting on One Foot

Do not be alarmed if you see your cockatiel occasionally resting on only one foot. This is normal behavior (the resting foot is often drawn up into the belly feathers). If you see your bird always using both feet to perch, please contact your avian veterinarian because this can indicate a health problem.

Screaming

Well-cared-for cockatiels will vocalize quietly, but birds who feel neglected and have little attention paid to them may become screamers. Once a bird becomes a screamer, it can be a difficult habit to break, particularly since the bird feels rewarded with your negative attention every time he screams. You may not think that yelling angrily at your bird is a reward, but at least the bird gets to see you and to hear from you as you tell him (often in a loud, dramatic way) to be quiet.

Remember to give your bird regular, consistent attention (at least thirty minutes a day), provide him with an interesting environment, including a variety of toys, feed him a well-balanced diet, and leave a radio or television on when you're away to provide background noise, and your bird shouldn't become a screamer.

Sneezing

In pet birds, sneezes are classified as either nonproductive or productive. Nonproductive sneezes clear a bird's nares (what we think of as nostrils) and are nothing to worry about. Some birds even stick a claw into their nares to induce a sneeze from time to time, much as a snuff dipper takes a pinch to produce the same effect. Productive sneezes, on the other hand, produce a discharge and are a cause for concern. If your bird sneezes frequently and you see a discharge from his nares or notice that the area around his nares is wet, contact your avian veterinarian immediately to set up an appointment to have your bird's health checked.

Abnormal Behaviors

If your cockatiel shows signs of any of the following behaviors, make an appointment with your avian veterinarian because they can indicate illness in a pet bird.

- Sleeping too much
- Sitting with feathers fluffed for long periods of time, even on warm days
- Listlessness
- Lack of appetite
- Regurgitating whole seeds
- Loss of balance or inability to perch
- Feather picking
- Feather chewing

Tasting/Testing Things with the Beak

Birds use their beaks and mouths to explore their world, in much the same way people use their hands. For example, don't be surprised if your cockatiel reaches out to tentatively taste or bite your hand before stepping onto it the first time. Your bird isn't biting you to be mean; he's merely investigating his world and testing the strength of a new perch using the tools he has available.

Thrashing

Cockatiels, particularly lutinos, seem prone to a condition that is described as "night frights," "cockatiel thrashing syndrome," or "earthquake syndrome." Birds who have thrashing episodes will be startled from sleep by loud noises or vibrations that cause them to awaken suddenly and try to take flight. In the case of caged pet birds, the thrasher may injure his wing tips, feet, chest, or abdomen on toys or cage bars when he tries to flee from the perceived danger.

Bird owners can help protect their pets from harm by installing a small night-light near the bird's cage to help the bird see where he is during a thrashing episode, by placing an air cleaner in the bird's room to provide white noise that will drown out some potentially frightening background noises, or by placing the bird in a small sleeping cage at night that is free of toys and other items that could harm a frightened bird.

Birds use their beaks and mouths to explore their world.

Feathered Warnings

Your bird's feathers are one of the most fascinating organs of his body. The bird uses feathers for movement, warmth, and balance, among other things. The following are some feather-related behaviors that can indicate health problems.

- **Fluffing:** A healthy cockatiel will fluff before preening or for short periods. If your cockatiel seems to remain fluffed up for an extended period, see your avian veterinarian. This can be a sign of illness.
- **Mutual preening:** Two birds will preen each other affectionately, but if you notice excessive feather loss, make sure one bird is not picking on the other and pulling out healthy feathers.
- **Feather picking:** A healthy bird will preen often to keep his feathers in top shape. However, a bird under stress may start to preen excessively, and severe feather loss can result.

Threats

If your cockatiel wants to threaten a cagemate, another pet in the home, or one of his human companions, he will stand as tall as he can with his crest raised halfway and his mouth open. He will also try to bite the object of his threats.

Vocalization

Many parrots vocalize around sunrise and sunset, which I believe hearkens back to flock behavior in the wild when parrots call to each other to start and end their days. You may notice that your pet cockatiel calls to you when you are out of the room. This may mean he feels lonely or that he needs some reassurance from you. Call back to him from the other room to tell him he's fine and that he's being a good bird, and he should settle down and begin playing or eating. If he continues to call to you, however, you may want to check on him to make sure everything is all right in his world.

Stress

This can show itself in many ways in your bird's behavior, including shaking, diarrhea, rapid breathing, wing and tail fanning, screaming, feather picking, poor sleeping habits, and loss of appetite. Over a period of time, stress can harm your parakeet's health.

To prevent your bird from becoming stressed, try to provide him with as normal and regular a routine as possible. Parrots are, for the most part, creatures of habit, and they don't always adapt well to sudden changes in their environment or schedule. If you do have to change something, talk to your parrot about it first. I know it seems crazy, but telling your bird what you're going to do before you do it may actually help reduce his stress. I received this advice from avian behaviorist Christine Davis, and now I explain what I'm doing every time I rearrange the living room or leave my bird at the vet's office for boarding during business trips. If you're going to be away on vacation, tell your bird how long you'll be gone and count the days out on your fingers in front of the bird or show him a calendar.

Chapter 10

Having Fun with Your Cockatiel

Now that you've learned the basics of caring for your new cockatiel, it's time to really enjoy your pet's companionship. Try to spend time with your bird each day to make sure her emotional needs for companionship and stimulation are being met. Remember that you and your family are substituting for your cockatiel's flock and that your cockatiel is a very social little bird who needs companionship regularly to feel secure and content in her surroundings.

To make spending time with your pet each day a true pleasure, it's best to train her to follow simple commands that make her easier to handle. This way, you can take your cockatiel with you while you are doing homework, talking on the phone, or watching television. Your bird will benefit from the time spent with you outside her cage, and you will have more time to enjoy her. Whenever your cockatiel is out of her cage, be sure to supervise her carefully to ensure she stays safe and healthy! (See chapter 5 for tips on household safety.)

Taming Your Cockatiel

Taming a parrot was one of the most popular topics of discussion when I worked at *Bird Talk,* and the discussion continues today between avian behaviorists and their clients in bird club meetings, books and magazine articles, and on the Internet.

A good first step in taming your cockatiel is getting her to be comfortable around you. To do this, give your bird a bit of warning before you approach her cage. Don't sneak up on her and try not to startle her. Call her name when you walk into the room. Try to be quiet and move slowly around your pet. Keep your hands behind you and reassure the bird that you aren't there to harm her, that everything is all right, and that she's a wonderful cockatiel.

After your bird is comfortable having you in the same room, try placing your hand in her cage as a first step toward taking her out. Just rest your hand in the cage, on the floor, or on a perch, and hold it there for a few seconds. Don't be surprised if your bird flutters around and squawks at first at the "intruder."

Do this several times each day, leaving your hand in the cage for slightly longer each day. Within a few days, your cockatiel won't make a fuss about your hand being in her space, and she may come over to investigate this new perch. Do not remove your hand from the birdcage the first time your cockatiel lands on it; just let her get used to perching on your hand.

After your cockatiel has calmly perched on your hand for several days in a row, try to take your hand out of the cage slowly with your bird on it. Some cockatiels will take to this new adventure willingly, while others are reluctant to leave the safety and security of home. (Be sure your bird's wings are clipped, as explained in chapter 7, and all doors and windows are secured before taking your bird out of her cage.)

The first step in taming your cockatiel is to teach her to perch on your hand for her trip into and out of her cage.

If your bird doesn't seem to like this at all, you can try an alternate taming method. Take the bird out of her cage and into a small room, such as a bathroom, that has been bird-proofed (the toilet lid is down, the shower door is closed, all windows are closed, and the bathroom hasn't been recently cleaned with any cleansers that have strong chemical odors). Sit down on the floor, place your bird in front of you, and begin gently playing with her. Don't be surprised if your bird tries to fly a few times. With clipped wings, however, she won't get very far and will give up trying after a few failed attempts.

Breeder Charlene Beane has demonstrated her parakeet taming method for me several times, and its simplicity and effectiveness always amazes me. I'm sure the same process can be used to calm cockatiels, too. Charlene will hold a bird who isn't quite tame close to her chest so the bird can hear her heartbeat, which seems to calm the bird. She then talks to the bird in a low, soothing tone and explains that the bird will make someone a wonderful pet. As she does this, she gently begins to stroke the cockatiel's back, which helps the bird relax. She continues for about five minutes to explain the bird's role as a perfect pet, stroking the bird as she talks. Pretty soon, the bird is calm and ready to be handled.

Step Up, Step Down

Once you've calmed your cockatiel using Charlene's method, see if you can make perching on your hand a game for your pet. Once she masters perching on your hand, you can teach her to step up by gently pressing your finger up and into the bird's belly. This will cause the bird to step up. As she does so, say "step up" or "up." Before long, your bird will respond to this command without much prompting.

Along with the "up" command, you may want to teach your cockatiel the "down" command. When you put the bird down on her cage or playgym, simply say "down" as she steps off your hand. These two simple commands give you a great deal of control over your bird, because you can say "up" to put an unruly bird back in her cage and you can tell a parrot who needs to go to bed "down" as you put the bird in her cage at night.

After your bird has mastered the "up" and "down" commands, encourage her to climb a "ladder" by moving her from index finger to index finger (the "rungs"). Keep taming sessions short (about ten minutes is the maximum cockatiel attention span) and make them fun so taming is enjoyable for both of you.

Teach your bird to step up onto your hand from a perch.

Petting

After your bird has become comfortable sitting on your hand, try petting her. Birds seem to like to have their heads, backs, cheek patches, under wing areas, and eye areas (including the closed eyelids) scratched or petted lightly. Quite a few like to have a spot low on their back at the base of their tail (over their preen glands) rubbed. Many birds do not enjoy having their stomachs scratched, although yours may think this is heaven! You'll have to experiment to see where your bird likes to be petted. You'll know you're successful if your bird clicks or grinds her beak, pins her eyes, or settles onto your hand or your lap with a completely relaxed, blissful expression on her face.

Some people may try to tell you that you need to wear gloves while taming your cockatiel to protect yourself from a bite. I recommend against this. A cockatiel generally doesn't bite *that* hard, and wearing gloves will only make your hands appear scarier to your bird. If your pet is scared, taming her will take more time and patience on your part, which may make the process less enjoyable for you both.

Toilet Training

Although some people don't believe it, cockatiels and other parrots can be toilet trained so they don't eliminate on their owners. If you want to toilet train your bird, you will have to choose a word or phrase that will mean the act of eliminating to your pet, such as "poop" or "go potty." While you're training your pet to associate the word or phrase with the action, you will have to train yourself to recognize what body language and actions indicate your cockatiel is about to eliminate, such as shifting around or squatting slightly. Use the phrase every time you see your cockatiel eliminate.

Once your bird seems to associate "go potty" with eliminating, you can try picking her up and holding her until she starts to shift or squat. Tell the bird to "go potty" while placing her on her cage, where she can eliminate. Once she's done, pick your bird up again and praise her for being such a smart bird!

Expect a few accidents while you are both learning this trick, but soon you'll have a toilet-trained bird: You can put her on her cage about every twenty minutes or so, give her the command, and expect the bird to eliminate on command.

Naughty Cockatiels

Training a cockatiel (or any bird) takes a great deal of time and patience. You must first gain your pet's trust, and then you must ensure you never lose it. To accomplish this, you must be careful not to lose your temper with your bird and *never* hit her. Birds are very sensitive, intelligent creatures who do not deserve to be hit, no matter how you may feel in a moment of anger.

Potty training your bird will make it much more pleasant to have her out in the house with you.

Although parrots are clever creatures, they are not linear "cause and effect" thinkers. If a parrot commits action A (chewing on some molding under your kitchen cabinets, for example), she won't associate reaction B (you yelling at her, locking her in her cage, or otherwise punishing her) with the misbehavior. As a result, most traditional forms of discipline are ineffective with parrots.

So what do you do when your cockatiel misbehaves? Try to catch her in the act. Look at your bird sternly and tell her "no" in a firm voice. If the bird is climbing or chewing on something she shouldn't, remove her from the source of danger and temptation as you tell her "no." If your bird has wound herself up into a screaming banshee, sometimes a short time-out in her cage with the cover on (between five and ten minutes will do in most cases) will do wonders to calm her down. Once the screaming stops and the bird has calmed down enough to play quietly, eat, or simply move around her cage, take the cover off to reveal a well-behaved, calm pet.

Will My Cockatiel Talk?

One of the most appealing aspects of cockatiel ownership is the possibility that your bird will become a talented talker. Although many cockatiels learn to talk, none of them is guaranteed to talk. The tips here will help you teach your cockatiel to talk, but please don't be disappointed if your bird never utters a word.

Remember that language, whether it's cockatiel or human, helps members of a species or group communicate. Most baby birds learn the language of their parents because it helps them communicate within their family and their flock. A pet cockatiel raised with people may learn to imitate the sounds she hears her human family make, but if you have more than one cockatiel the birds may find communicating with each other easier and more enjoyable than trying to learn your language.

Most experts say that the best time to teach a cockatiel to talk is between the time she leaves the nest and her first birthday. If you have an adult cockatiel, the chances of her learning to talk are less than if you start with a young bird. Male birds may be more likely to talk, but I have heard of some talkative females, too.

Talking Tips

You will be more successful in training a cockatiel to talk if you keep a single pet bird, rather than a pair. Birds kept in pairs or groups are more likely to bond with other birds than with people. By the same token, don't give your bird any toys with mirrors on them if you want the bird to learn to talk, since your bird will think the bird in the mirror is a potential cagemate with whom she can bond.

Dr. Irene Pepperberg and Alex

An African grey parrot named Alex, who is being studied by Irene M. Pepperberg, PhD, at the University of Arizona, has a hundred-word vocabulary, can count to six, and can correctly answer questions about the size, shape, color, and number of objects shown him. He can categorize objects, telling a ques-

common or how they

the bird is, the more likely she

ockatiel to whistle if you want
bird to learn than talking, and
n't learn to talk. If you do want
neone who whistles well train
result, rather than being stuck
istler over and over again.
and simple, such as the bird's
it clearly. Some people teach
d phrases quickly, only to be
ılurred jumble that cannot be

Be sure to say the chosen phrase with emphasis and enthusiasm. Birds like drama, and seem to learn words that are said emphatically—which may be why some of them pick up bad language so quickly!

Try to use phrases that make sense in context. For instance, say "good morning" or "hello" when you uncover the bird's cage each day. Say "good-bye" when you leave the room, or ask "want a treat?" when you offer your cockatiel her meals. Phrases that make sense are also more likely to be used by you and other members of your family when conversing with your bird. The more your bird hears an interesting word or phrase, the more likely she is to say that phrase some day.

Don't change the phrase around. If you're teaching your bird to say "hello," for example, don't say "hello" one day, then "hi" the next, followed by "hi, Petey!" (or whatever your bird's name is) another day.

Speak to your bird with enthusiasm—birds like drama.

Keep training sessions short. Cockatiel breeders recommend ten- to fifteen-minute sessions.

Train your bird in a quiet area. Think of how distracting it is when someone is trying to talk to you with a radio or television blaring in the background. It's hard to hear what the other person is saying under those conditions, isn't it? Your cockatiel won't be able to hear you any better or understand what you are trying to accomplish if you try to train her in the midst of noisy distractions. Be sure to keep your cockatiel involved in your family's routine, though, because isolating her completely won't help her feel comfortable and part of the family. Remember that a bird needs to feel comfortable in her environment before she will draw attention to herself by talking.

Be patient with your pet. Stop the sessions if you find you are getting frustrated. Your cockatiel will sense that something is bothering you and will react by becoming bothered herself. This is not an ideal situation for you or your bird. Try to keep your mood upbeat. Smile a lot and praise your pet when she does well!

Graduate to more difficult phrases as your bird masters simple words. Consider keeping a log of the words your bird knows. (This is especially helpful if more than one person will be working with the cockatiel.)

When you aren't talking to your cockatiel, try listening to her. Cockatiels and other birds sometimes mumble to themselves to practice talking as they drift off to sleep. Because a cockatiel has a very small voice, you'll have to listen carefully to hear if your pet is making progress.

You're probably wondering if the talking tapes and CDs sold in pet supply stores and through advertisements in bird magazines work. The most realistic answer I can give is "sometimes." Some birds learn from the repetition of the tapes and CDs that, fortunately, have gotten livelier and more interesting in recent years. Other birds benefit from having their owners make tapes of the phrases the bird is currently learning and hearing those tapes when their owners aren't around. I recommend against playing a constant barrage of taped phrases during the day, because the bird is likely to get bored hearing the same thing for hours on end. If she's bored, the bird will be more likely to tune out the tape and the training.

Finally, if your patient, consistent training seems to be going nowhere, you may have to accept the fact that your cockatiel isn't going to talk. Don't be too disappointed if your pet doesn't learn to talk. Most birds don't, and talking ability should never be the primary reason for owning a bird. If you end up with a nontalking pet, continue to love her for the unique creature she is.

The Trick to Training

One of the best ways to spend time with your cockatiel is to teach her to do simple tricks. Your bird will come to expect and enjoy the extra attention you give her during training sessions, and you will see a stronger bond develop between you and your bird as the training progresses.

Before you begin to teach your cockatiel tricks, make sure you have the patience and perseverance to undertake training sessions. Birds sometimes behave as we expect them to, but sometimes they want to do what they want to do, and it's up to you not to become frustrated or angry with your pet when she does not behave as you expect. Anger and frustration can damage the relationship you have with your bird, so be sure to be patient and cheerful during each training session.

As you begin to plan what tricks you will teach your cockatiel, notice what your bird likes to do and make it part of her trick training. You will soon find it's much easier to expand on one or more of your bird's natural behaviors, and that will make trick training easier and more enjoyable for both of you. For example, some cockatiels like to climb while others may enjoy holding their wings in the air and stretching (this can be turned into an eagle pose without too much effort). Others amuse themselves by using their beaks to examine a wide variety of items in their environment, and you can teach them to touch objects as you name them.

Reward your bird's efforts in training with food treats, praise, petting, and cuddling.

Tips for Better Training

To make the most of your parrot training sessions, keep the following points in mind.

Know what your bird likes and dislikes. If your bird is naturally playful, she will be a better candidate to learn tricks than a bird who is content to sit on her owner's hand for head scratching.

Provide several short training sessions each day. Pet birds have short attention spans, and they tend to become cranky if you try to teach them something once you've exceeded that attention span. Ten minutes or less, several times a day, is usually more effective than one longer session.

Make the sessions fun. Remember that these training sessions are supposed to be enjoyable for both you and your bird, and immediately end any session that is not going well.

Reward your bird's good behavior with a combination of food treats, verbal praise, petting, or cuddling. If your bird loves to have her head nape scratched, for instance, give this area extra attention when your bird performs her trick correctly. This way she will learn to respond to different types of rewards, rather than just waiting for a favorite food treat to come her way.

Appreciate your bird for the unique individual she is. Love your bird because she is your pet, not because of the tricks she can do. Some birds are natural show-offs, while others are more reserved. If you have a quick trick learner, teach the bird tricks and add to her repertoire over time. If your bird doesn't seem to enjoy learning tricks, don't force the issue. Appreciate your bird for all of her other wonderful qualities and love her as your pet.

> **TIP**
>
> **Trick Training Tips**
>
> Know what your bird likes and dislikes.
>
> Provide several short training sessions each day.
>
> Make the sessions fun.
>
> Appreciate your bird for the unique individual she is.

Tricks to Teach Your Cockatiel

Your cockatiel is a bright bird and can learn to perform a wide variety of tricks. Her repertoire of learned behaviors is limited only by your imagination and your patience during the training process. Listed below are some beginning tricks to teach your pet. As your training skills improve, you will undoubtedly come up with some tricks that are unique to you and your bird. Good luck, and remember to have fun!

Ride in a Wagon

A cockatiel who is outgoing and unafraid of new toys or new people is a good candidate to learn to ride in a wagon or even in a radio-controlled car. If your bird is shy, though, she may not enjoy riding in a toy vehicle, and you might want to try a different trick instead.

To teach your cockatiel to ride in a wagon, you must first get your bird accustomed to the vehicle. Roll the wagon or drive the car in front of your pet to show her what it will do. Praise the bird if she does not run away from the moving vehicle and reassure her that she will be okay if the vehicle motion seems frightening.

After a few days of short sessions of watching the wagon or car roll by, put your bird in the vehicle. Let her sit in it without moving the wagon. Praise and pet your cockatiel as she sits in the wagon, and continue to get the bird accustomed to the vehicle by letting her sit in it for brief periods over several days.

When your bird seems completely comfortable sitting in the wagon, move it a short distance. Praise your cockatiel for her good behavior if she sits calmly, or comfort and reassure your pet if she seems excited or anxious over the vehicle's movement. Put your bird in the vehicle for short rides several times a day, and gradually increase the length of time spent and distance traveled during the rides.

Nod Your Head

A cockatiel who interacts well with her owner and is unafraid of showing off for strangers is a good candidate to learn to nod her head yes and shake her head no.

To teach your bird to nod her head, hold a small portion of her favorite treat just out of reach of her beak and slowly bob it up and down. Your cockatiel will nod her head as she follows the motion of the treat, trying to catch it with her beak. Give her verbal praise, such as "is that a yes?" as she nods, so she will associate the words with the motion.

It's not hard to get your cockatiel to move her head as you move your hand. You can turn that behavior into a trick.

Practice this trick with the treat and the verbal praise, and gradually increase the praise while eliminating the treat.

To teach your cockatiel to shake her head no, repeat the steps above but move the treat side to side instead of up and down, so your bird's head will shake side to side to indicate no. Provide different verbal praise, such as "is that a no?" as you move the treat from side to side.

Pose Like an Eagle

A cockatiel who enjoys being petted under her wings is a very good candidate to learn to pose like an eagle. Birds who do not enjoy being petted under their wings can also learn this trick, but training them may take a little longer.

Start your training by gently tickling your cockatiel under each wing tip with your index finger. This will cause your cockatiel to raise her wings. Praise her at this point by saying something like "good eagle, good bird" so your cockatiel will begin to associate the word "eagle" with raising her wings.

Practice the combination of gentle tickling and verbal praise at each training session. Increase the use of verbal praise and decrease the tickling until your cockatiel responds to your words alone.

Drop Coins in a Bank

A cockatiel who enjoys picking things up with her beak is a good candidate to learn to drop coins in a bank. To perform this trick, you will need some clean cockatiel-sized coins (dimes work well) and a bank.

Put some clean dimes in front of your bird on a tabletop. Her curious nature will soon get the better of her and she will pick up a dime. When she does, praise her and reward her with a food treat.

Practice this behavior until the bird is comfortable picking up the coins, and gradually replace the food reward with verbal praise. After the bird is comfortable picking up the coins, drop a coin into the piggybank in front of the bird. When

This cockatiel can pose like an eagle while playing the organ. What a smart bird!

your bird tries to imitate your behavior, praise her and reward her with a food treat. Continue practicing the trick until your bird masters dropping the coins into the slot in the bank, and gradually replace the food treats with verbal praise. In no time at all, your bird should have the hang of making deposits into her own piggybank.

Traveling with Your Bird

When I worked for *Bird Talk,* we often heard from bird owners who wanted to take their pets on vacation and from people relocating to another state or country. The advice we gave them about traveling with their bird depended on the owner and their pet. These were some of the questions we asked:

Does the bird like new adventures?

Is there a trusted relative or friend you can leave the bird with while you are away?

Does your avian veterinarian's office offer boarding?

How long will you be gone?

Will you be visiting a foreign country?

Some birds are up for any adventure.

If the owners were going on a family vacation, we usually recommended leaving the bird at home in familiar surroundings with her own food, water, and cage or in the care of a trusted friend, relative, pet sitter, or avian veterinarian. We advised this because birds are creatures of habit who like their routines and because taking birds across state lines or international boundaries is not without risk. Some species are illegal in certain states (Quaker, or monk parakeets, for example, are believed to pose an agricultural threat to some states because of their hearty appetites), and some foreign countries require lengthy quarantine stays for pet birds. It was our professional opinion that, although it is difficult to leave your bird behind when you travel, it is better for the bird. (Of course, if you're moving, that's a different story!)

If you leave your pet at home while you're away, you have several care options. First, you can recruit the services of a trusted friend or relative, which is an inexpensive and convenient solution for many pet owners. You can return the pet-sitting favor when your friend or relative goes out of town.

If your trusted friends and relatives live far away, you can hire a professional pet sitter (many advertise in the Yellow Pages, and some offer additional services such as picking up mail, watering your plants, and leaving lights and/or radios on to make your home seem occupied while you're gone). If you're not sure about what to look for in a pet sitter, the National Association of Professional Pet Sitters offers the following tips:

TIP

Finding a Bird Sitter

National Association of Professional Pet Sitters, (800) 296-PETS, www.petsitters.org

Pet Sitters International, (800) 268-SITS, www.petsit.com

- Look for a bonded pet sitter who carries commercial liability insurance.
- Ask for references and for a written description of services and fees.
- Arrange to have the pet sitter come to your home before you leave on your trip to meet the pets and to discuss what services you would like them to perform while you're away.
- During the initial interview, evaluate the sitter. Do they seem comfortable with your bird? Does the sitter have experience caring for birds? Do they own birds?
- Ask for a written contract and discuss the availability of vet care (do they have an existing arrangement with your veterinarian, for example) and what arrangements the sitter makes in the event of inclement weather or personal illness.
- Discuss the sitter's policy for making sure you have returned home. Should you call them to confirm your arrival, or will they call you?

If the prospect of leaving your bird with a pet sitter doesn't appeal to you, you may be able to board your bird at your avian veterinarian's office. Of course, you'll need to find out if your vet's office offers boarding services and decide if you want to risk your bird's health by exposing her to other birds during boarding.

Appendix

Learning More About Your Cockatiel

Some Good Books

Alderton, David, *You and Your Pet Bird*, Alfred A. Knopf, 1994.
Forshaw, Joseph, *Parrots of the World*, TFH Publications, 1977.
Grindol, Diane, *The Complete Book of Cockatiels,* Howell Book House, 1998.
Spadafori, Gina, and Brian L. Speer, DVM, *Birds for Dummies,* Wiley, 1999.

About Health Care

Doane, Bonnie Munro, *The Parrot in Health and Illness: An Owner's Guide,* Howell Book House, 1991.
Gallerstein, Gary A., DVM, *The Complete Bird Owner's Handbook,* Avian Publications, 2003.
McCluggage, David, DVM, and Pamela L. Higdon. *Holistic Care for Birds,* Howell Book House, 1999.
Rach, Julie, and Gallerstein, Gary A., DVM, *First Aid for Birds: An Owner's Guide to a Happy Healthy Pet,* Howell Book House, 1998.

About Training

Athan, Mattie Sue, *Guide to a Well-Behaved Parrot,* Barron's, 1993.
Doane, Bonnie Munro, and Thomas Qualkinbush, *My Parrot, My Friend,* Howell Book House, 1994.

Grindol, Diane, and Tom Roudybush, *Teaching Your Bird to Talk,* Howell Book House, 2003.
Hubbard, Jennifer, *The New Parrot Training Handbook: A Complete Guide to Taming and Training Your Pet Bird,* Parrot Press, 1997.
Rach, Julie, *Why Does My Bird Do That?,* Howell Book House, 1998.

Magazines

Bird Talk
Monthly magazine devoted to pet bird ownership.
Subscription information: P.O. Box 57347, Boulder, CO 80322-7347
www.birdtalkmagazine.com

Birds USA
Annual magazine aimed at first-time bird owners.
Look for it in your local bookstore or pet supply store.
www.birdtalkmagazine.com

Bird Times
This magazine for pet bird owners is published six times a year.
Subscription information: Pet Publishing, Inc. 7-L Dundas Circle, Greensboro, NC 27407
www.petpublishing.com/birdtimes/

Online Resources

Bird-specific sites have been cropping up regularly on the Internet. These sites offer pet bird owners the opportunity to share stories about their pets and trade helpful hints about bird care.

To find an avian veterinarian, visit the **Association of Avian Veterinarians** at www.aav.org. To find a holistic avian veterinarian in your area, visit the **American Holistic Veterinary Medical Association** at www.ahvma.org. Both sites offer ways to search for practitioners in your area.

American Cockatiel Society
www.acstiels.com

American Animal Hospital Association
www.healthypet.com

American Veterinary Medical Association
www.avma.org/care4pets/

National Cockatiel Society
www.cockatiels.org/

Online Pet Cockatiel Questions
www.cockatiels.org/ncs/features/petcare.html

Photo Credits:
Diane Grindol: 4–5, 8–9, 11, 15, 16, 19, 20, 21, 22, 26, 32, 35, 44, 47, 50, 53, 64, 65, 67, 68, 72, 82, 88, 92, 99, 104, 108, 114, 120
John Tyson Photography: 1, 13, 24, 28–29, 30, 31, 34, 38, 41, 42, 46, 49, 51, 55, 57, 58, 59, 60, 61, 70, 73, 77, 79, 84, 85, 86, 89, 95, 96–97, 98, 100, 101, 102, 107, 110, 111, 116, 118, 119
David Wrobel: 40

Index